H. d Toulouse Lautrec

'H. d Toulouse Lautrec

LESLEY STEVENSON

Weidenfeld and Nicolson, London

Illustration p. 3
Henri de Toulouse-Lautrec, 1896
Drawing, 10 x 9 cm
Albi, Musée Toulouse-Lautrec

First published in Great Britain in 1991 by
George Weidenfeld & Nicolson Limited
91 Clapham High Street, London SW4 7TA

Written by Lesley Stevenson in association with
First Edition Translations Ltd, Cambridge.

Coordination and production: Smeets Illustrated Projects, Weert
Phototypesetting: Royal Smeets Offset, Weert
Print: Royal Smeets Offset b.v., Weert, The Netherlands

ISBN 0 297 83124 0

Contents

Chronology

1864	Henri-Marie-Raymond de Toulouse-Lautrec-Monfa born 24 November, son of Adèle-Zoë née Tapié de Céleyran (1841–1930) and Comte Alphonse-Charles de Toulouse-Lautrec-Monfa (1838–1912) at the Château du Bosc in Albi.
1872	Goes with the Comtesse to Paris to begin his education at the Lycée Fontanes. Meets Maurice Joyant.
1875	Returns to Albi where he is educated by private tutors.
1878	Breaks left leg.
1879	Breaks right leg.
1881	Fails baccalauréat in July, passes in November.
1882	Goes to Paris to start studying painting with René Princeteau. Joins Léon Bonnat's studio in March and when it closes in September goes to Fernand Cormon's where he meets Louis Anquetin, René Grenier, Emile Bernard and, in 1886, Vincent Van Gogh.
1883	The Comtesse buys the Château de Malromé.
1884	Lodges with the Greniers in Paris.
1885	Becomes a regular at Aristide Bruant's cabaret Le Mirliton. Meets Suzanne Valadon.
1886	The Mirliton starts exhibiting his works. Takes a studio on the rue Caulaincourt/rue Tourlaque. Stops attending Cormon's on a regular basis.
1887	Lives with Dr Henri Bourges. Meets Théo Van Rysselberghe.
1888	Exhibits eleven paintings and one drawing with Les XX in Brussels and at the Salon des Indépendants in Paris.
1889	The Exposition Universelle in Paris. Lautrec exhibits at the Cercle Volney and at the Salon des Indépendants: *Moulin de la Galette*.
1890	Exhibits once again with Les XX and goes to Brussels, the Salon des Indépendants, and the Cercle Volney. Goes to Biarritz and San Sebastian. Joyant succeeds Theo Van Gogh at Goupil's gallery.
1891	Begins to produce lithographs. Zidler commissions *At the Moulin Rouge: La Goulue* from him. Exhibits at the Salon des Indépendants, Cercle Volney and Le Barc de Boutteville. His cousin Gabriel Tapié de Céleyran arrives in Paris to practise medicine.
1892	Exhibits with Les XX, Cercle Volney, the Salon des Indépendants and Le Barc de Boutteville. Visits London. Decorates Salon of rue d'Amboise brothel.
1893	Exhibits with Les XX, at Boussod Valadon (through Joyant), at the Indépendants. After Bourges' marriage, he moves in with his mother. Works for the *Figaro Illustré*, which is issued by Valadon, for the *Revue Blanche* and *L'Escarmouche*.

1894	Travels to Belgium, Holland and London. Exhibits at Durand-Ruel's and the Royal Aquarium in London.
1895	Exhibits with La Libre Esthétique in Brussels.
	Travels to London where he meets Whistler and Oscar Wilde. Exhibits at the Royal Aquarium.
	In Paris exhibits at the Indépendants, the Salon de la Société Nationale des Beaux-Arts, the Centenaire de la Lithographie, the Salon des Cent and the Manzi-Joyant gallery, where two rooms are closed to the public.
	Sets out from Le Havre and sails to Arcachon. Goes to Lisbon and Madrid with Maurice Guibert.
1896	Exhibits at La Libre Esthétique, the Indépendants, Salon des Cent (the *Elles* series) and at the Manzi-Joyant gallery.
	Goes to San Sebastian, Burgos, Madrid and Toledo.
1897	Exhibits at La Libre Esthétique and the Indépendants. Travels to London. Moves to the avenue Frochot studio.
1898	Exhibits seventy-eight works in Goupil's London gallery.
1899	Is hospitalised in Dr Sémelaigne's sanatorium in Neuilly because of his alcoholism.
	In May he goes to Albi, on a cruise from Le Havre to Bordeaux, and then to his mother's home at Malromé.
	In October acts as a member of the jury for the lithographic section at the Exposition Universelle.
1900	Visits Malromé and stays in Bordeaux.
1901	At Bordeaux and Malromé.
	After winding up his affairs in Paris, goes to Malromé where he dies on 9 September.

Self-Portrait, 1880
Cardboard, 40.3 x 32.4 cm
Albi, Musée Toulouse-Lautrec

Foreword

The public versus the private

The appeal of Toulouse-Lautrec, one of the best-known nineteenth-century French artists, has endured in a way that marks him off from those of his contemporaries who also practised painting and print-making in Paris. However, it is not simply his work that fascinates but the strange facts of his biography, which have helped enlarge his reputation. Indeed, much of the emphasis on his private life has been distorted and has often been studied to the detriment of his work. For example, in John Huston's 1953 award-winning biopic of the life of Lautrec, *Moulin Rouge*, the artist's romantic liaisons are filmed against the backdrop of the cabarets of nineteenth-century Montmartre. José Ferrer is Lautrec, a role which he played on his knees in order to accentuate the difference between the artist and the 'normal' people around him. In a sense, that otherness is the theme of the film – the artist is different because of his physical deformity, but also because of the genius that sets him apart from those who surround him. Four years later, Vincente Minnelli's *Lust for Life* explored the same archetypal relationship between the artist and society, focusing this time on the life of Van Gogh.

The comparison between these two artists, who met briefly in 1886, is worth exploring because both became public property via the movie industry. In both films the mythologisation of the artist is taken to extremes. The cult of the romantic artist, begun in the early nineteenth century, invests the artist's personal life with as much significance as his work, and in the film the work stands for the personality. It is no coincidence that both artists were perceived as mad (a matter of no little embarrassment to their respectable families) and that the sad facts of their personalities were exploited by film-makers and biographers, to consummate their artistic martyrdoms. Often incidental anecdotal elements are invested with a far greater significance than they merit, and the spectator's overriding memory is of Toulouse-Lautrec's grossly deformed body, and of Van Gogh's self-mutilation. Much of the films' drama derives from these personal tragedies. Both artists are shown as being alienated from their families and from their peers (whether because of their 'madness' or their 'genius'); and indeed alienation becomes a kind of pre-requisite for entry to the avant-garde.

Yet against this public façade any reading of the correspondence of Van Gogh or Toulouse-Lautrec reveals a quite different private figure. Both enjoyed close, if equivocal, relationships with their families, and their letters reveal the monotonous realities of daily life in the nineteenth century rather than any great artistic achievements. In their late thirties both artists were still dependent on their families for money (albeit for different reasons) and their loving letters often end with an urgent plea for cash. It is clear that both Van Gogh's brother and Toulouse-Lautrec's mother were often only

At Chantilly Races, 1879
Canvas, 47 x 58 cm
Private collection

Horse-woman followed by her Groom, 1880
Panel, 14.1 x 23.4 cm
Albi, Musée Toulouse-Lautrec

too happy to subsidise their activities if it meant keeping the socially embarrassing artists at bay. Theo Van Gogh bought Gauguin's companionship for his brother in Arles, at a safe distance from his burgeoning activities as a respectable art dealer in Paris. The Comtesse de Toulouse-Lautrec fled Paris, leaving her son a bribe of 1,000 francs when his strange behaviour became unbearable. It is little wonder that both artists are perceived as being in combat with bourgeois respectability in their art as much as in their lives.

It is also often suggested that both artists died at the age of 37, enhancing an impression of artistic martyrdom – another pre-requisite of genius seems to be an early death – and of a career left sadly unfinished. By the time of their respective deaths, however, both were aged and worn down by the twin evils of nineteenth-century bohemia: alcoholism and syphilis. Toulouse-Lautrec was in fact only 36.

Of course, their lives and their art were different in many important respects. Lautrec never experienced real financial difficulties: he came from a wealthy, aristocratic family and it was only his spendthrift nature that caused him to have to borrow money from his friends and family. Unlike Van Gogh, or indeed other vanguard artists such as the Impressionists before him, he enjoyed real success in his twenties, so much so that in 1892 he won a legal case against forgers of his work. Not only did he enjoy financial success but the critical success which eluded Van Gogh during his lifetime was accorded to him. This difference in attitude towards their work could have derived from the increasing popularity of the print, at which medium Lautrec excelled, and his accessible subject-matter as much as from an essentially conservative style. That style derived from his immediate artistic antecedents and from Japanese art rather than from any real artistic innovation on Lautrec's part.

Both *Moulin Rouge* and *Lust for Life* exploit and uphold the romantic notion of the freedom of the artist, using it synecdochically to embody the freedom of a society. The fact that these two films were made during the Cold War is not coincidental and reveals as much about post-war emotions as about life in late nineteenth-century France. The worlds that are presented in the films are escapist and nostalgic, and a sense of *fin-de-siècle* decadence pervades both, portraying a libertarian society perched on the cusp of decline. The artists are located in environments to which they are strangers. Toulouse-Lautrec, the aristocrat from the south of France who spoke the Gascon dialect fluently, is transplanted into the seedy dance-halls of the capital, living in a political milieu which would have shocked his conservative family. He mixes freely with prostitutes and other characters on the fringes of society, and indeed derives inspiration from their liberating lifestyle. The *naïveté* and ambition of both films locates them firmly in another age, but the image of the artist that each conveys has persisted, so much so that it is now impossible to distinguish the legend from the history.

However, it is not only recent biographers and critics who have distorted the facts of Lautrec's life. Much of his posthumous reputation was established during his lifetime, and contemporary commentators writing in 1899 perceived both the artist and his work as embodying current fashions in a way that set him apart from his peers. Many of his prints and paintings represent topical subject-matter, particularly the scenes of café life and brothels, but it was far from being unique. Other current issues do not feature at all in his work, and he can never really be accorded the status of social commentator that could be used to describe artists of the previous generation such as Courbet or Manet. If anything, Lautrec's work can at best be held to encapsulate a sense of hedonism as France edged towards the new century. Neither was he alone in capturing that *Zeitgeist*. It seems rather as if Lautrec became the archetypal *fin-de-siècle* artist because the facts of his personal life rather than his work made him pre-eminently suitable for that kind of artistic martyrdom.

*Old Woman Sitting on a
Bench at Céleyran*, 1882
Canvas, 55 x 46 cm
Albi, Musée Toulouse-Lautrec

Seated Nude, 1882
Canvas, 55 x 46 cm
Albi, Musée Toulouse-Lautrec

16

Chapter 1

Early life

Henri-Marie-Raymond de Toulouse-Lautrec-Monfa was born on 24 November 1864 in the Château du Bosc, his mother's family home in Albi in south-western France. His mother, née Adèle-Zoë Tapié de Céleyran (1841–1930), had married his father Alphonse-Charles de Toulouse-Lautrec-Monfa (1838–1912) on 9 May 1863. They were first cousins.

The position of the aristocracy in France during the Second Empire and the Third Republic was an equivocal one, as the country industrialised and edged towards democracy. On the one hand the aristocracy continued to enjoy remarkable wealth and privilege, but they ceased to wield the political power that had been enjoyed by their ancestors. One of the effects of this uncertain existence was the incidence of intermarriage as aristocratic families tried to protect their wealth and status. Lautrec's father was a fervent horseman and his time seems to have been filled with such pursuits as hunting. This hobby became his sole *raison d'être* and he seems to have lost interest in his son after it became apparent that he would not continue the family equestrian tradition.

Despite industrialisation and improved communications, France was still far from being a unified country and the differences between the various regions continued to be very marked. Like Cézanne and Bazille, Toulouse-Lautrec was proud of his southern heritage; he could trace his family back to the Middle Ages and often spoke and wrote in the Gascon dialect. However, this never permeated his art.

The family was politically conservative. The young Lautrec wrote to his grandmother that they celebrated the Feast of Saint Louis each year on 25 August. This was his grandmother's feast day, but the nationalist and royalist implications of the date would not have been lost on the French aristocracy. Despite increasing secularisation in France, Toulouse-Lautrec's upbringing was Catholic, as much because of the family's desire to preserve the status quo and its royalist sympathies as from any real sense of piety. Letters to his godmother report his observance of saints' days and the celebration of his first communion in Paris in 1876. There is little to suggest that Toulouse-Lautrec ever deviated from his family's right-wing, nationalist, monarchic sentiments, and it was with some embarrassment that he reported to his mother in 1892 about a favourable review in a journal: 'The "Paris" a very republican newspaper (say nothing about it to the family) ...' At the same time, however, he mixed freely with republicans and anarchists in Montmartre, even during the Dreyfus scandal which polarised France between 1894 and 1906.

His parents had one other child, Richard-Constantin, who was born in 1867 and died just before his first birthday. After 1868 his parents effectively led separate lives. The Comte continued to hunt

The Artist's Mother at Breakfast, 1881
Canvas, 93.5 x 81 cm
Albi, Musée Toulouse-Lautrec

Comte Alphonse de Toulouse-
Lautrec as a Falconer, 1881
Panel, 23.5 x 14 cm
Albi, Musée Toulouse-Lautrec

Le Bosc, Artillery, 1879
Canvas, 64 x 49 cm
Albi, Musée Toulouse-Lautrec

The Comtesse de Toulouse-Lautrec
in the Salon at Malromé, 1887
Canvas, 59 x 54 cm
Albi, Musée Toulouse-Lautrec

and enjoy liaisons with other women, while his mother became increasingly pious and involved with her immediate family. Theirs was essentially a marriage of convenience, forged to consolidate family wealth and property. Indeed, intermarriage within the family was not unique to them: their siblings married each other and several of the resulting children did not survive infancy or were mentally retarded, the effects of their common genetic inheritance.

In 1872 the Comtesse took her son to Paris and they lodged in the Hôtel Pérey, near the faubourg Saint-Honoré, with occasional visits from the Comte. Lautrec attended the Lycée Fontanes (later the Lycée Condorcet) where he met Maurice Joyant (1864–1930), his life-long friend. Summers were spent in the south, and letters home record his homesickness. After a couple of years in the capital, Lautrec and his mother returned to Albi because of worries about his health. Thereafter, he was educated at home by his mother and a number of tutors.

In 1878 Toulouse-Lautrec broke his left leg. The following year he fractured the other one and neither leg grew after this time. Rather than the result of bad luck, this was most probably the effect of a pathological weakness caused by the rare hereditary bone disease pyknodysostosis, which is exacerbated by intermarriage and becomes apparent only during adolescence. As well as the characteristic short limbs, Lautrec manifested other symptoms such as the enlarged nostrils and lips that contemporaries commented upon.

With one son dead and the other's deformity representing so many frustrated hopes, any suggestion that his short stature was caused by a congenital weakness would have been a source of great guilt and embarrassment for his family. It was all too convenient to blame his distorted body on the successive falls, and understandable to attempt to find a cure. The following three winters were spent in the mild climate of Nice, and the Comtesse and her son took the waters at a number of spas. In addition, a number of alternative treatments were tried, but Toulouse-Lautrec never grew beyond five feet tall. In fact, he was still taller than the minimum required height for military service, but in the spring of 1884 he wrote to his mother that he had been declared unfit, without having to undergo any medical examination.

In 1880, after it had become apparent that Toulouse-Lautrec would not recover from his disease, he painted *Self-Portrait* (see p. 8), in which the adolescent youth is depicted looking in a mirror, presumably above a mantelpiece on which are placed various pieces of ceramic ware, a snuffed candle and a clock. It is the only self-portrait in oils in which he is depicted alone, and it represents a serious attempt not only to capture a likeness but also to record an adolescent's questioning. Later self-portraits are often caricatural in nature and deliberately mock his distorted body, apparently avoiding the issues that are confronted here.

He has not flattered himself. Heavy chiaroscuro means that half the face is in darkness, and the obscuring of the eyes is reminiscent of early self-portraits by Rembrandt. Already a few wisps of hair are growing on his chin, presaging the luxuriant beard which he was to grow a couple of years later, not only as an ironic sign of his virility but also in an attempt to disguise the rather full rosy

Emile Bernard, 1885
Canvas, 54.5 x 44 cm
London, Tate Gallery

lips which are evident here. The figure is small against a pale grey background that heightens his sense of isolation, and the candle and the clock serve as *momento mori*, being traditional allusions to the brevity of life. The handling of the paint is confident and along with the introspective nature of the picture, represents the work of a talented student.

Lautrec had already been drawing for some years and his youthful letters were decorated with sketches. Other members of his family enjoyed painting and his earliest oils reveal that he shared their interest in equestrian subjects; examples are the romantic portrait of his father with his falcon (see p. 18) and *At Chantilly Races* (see p. 10), in which he has captured a sense of movement in the rapidly applied impasto. This skill in capturing the moment in a kind of visual shorthand was to contribute to the success of his later cabaret works, which rely on similarly energetic subject-matter being treated with great fluency. Gradually, however, he began to depart from the area of horses and hunting, perhaps as a sign of his growing independence and perhaps also as a reaction against riding, which he could no longer enjoy. *Old Woman Sitting on a Bench at Céleyran* (see p. 14) is a remarkably sympathetic portrayal of one of the inhabitants of the family estate.

To Paris

In July 1881 Lautrec failed his baccalauréat examination, but he passed it at the second attempt in November of that year. Thereafter he abandoned his formal education and the following March he set off to Paris to train as a painter with René Princeteau (1839–1914) at 233 faubourg Saint-Honoré. A work such as *The Artist's Mother at Breakfast* (see p. 16) demonstrates how his art had matured from the *Self-Portrait* of 1880. The heavy chiaroscuro and thick paint

Fernand Cormon in his atelier
with among others
Toulouse-Lautrec, Emile Bernard,
Louis Anquetin,
Gustave Dennery and René
Grenier, 1885

23

Vincent Van Gogh, 1887
Cardboard, 54 x 45 cm
Amsterdam, Vincent Van Gogh
Foundation,
Rijksmuseum Vincent Van Gogh

Edgar Degas, 1834-1917
L'Absinthe, 1876
Canvas, 92 x 68 cm
Paris, Musée d'Orsay

have disappeared, and in its light tonality and the network of rapidly executed lines the painting is much closer in handling to the work of someone like Berthe Morisot or even to the work of the popular Salon painter Bastien-Lepage. Early portraits of his father, such as the contemporary *Comte Alphonse de Toulouse-Lautrec as a Falconer* (see p. 18), show him out of doors astride a horse, but his mother is always located within a domestic environment and she appears withdrawn and introspective, as in *The Comtesse de Toulouse-Lautrec in the Salon at Malromé* of 1887 (see p. 20). Of course, these were well–established gender roles which were not unique to the aristocracy, but they do serve to emphasise the incompatibility of the artist's parents.

By this time, it must have become evident to Lautrec's parents that he would never fulfil their ambitions by becoming an enthusiastic horseman, and his move to Paris must have seemed an ideal solution. That his art was regarded mainly as a dilettante pursuit, typical of a leisured young man in the French capital, is made clear by the choice of teacher. Princeteau, a friend of the Comte, was

Artilleryman and Woman, 1886
Paper, 57.8 x 46.2 cm
Albi, Musée Toulouse-Lautrec

a deaf mute who specialised in the genre known as *animaliers* (animal subjects), although he also painted straight genre scenes and did some history painting and a little sculpture. However, it was the scenes of hunting and riding for which he was best known, and the Comte presumably imagined that his son would continue the family tradition by concentrating on equestrian subjects. A number of Toulouse-Lautrec's works at this time show the influence of his teacher, both in choice of subject and technique.

Paris during the 1880s had begun to recover some of the optimism that had vanished with the defeat of the Franco-Prussian War and the effects of the bloody Commune. The changes to the city that had been made by Haussmann brought the new wide boulevards, pavements and street lighting that encouraged the growth of open-air cafés and places of entertainment. The faubourg Saint-Honoré, where Princeteau had his studio, was adjacent to the rue Saint-Honoré, where the Impressionist painters were having their seventh exhibition that spring. Here, Lautrec could have seen the best collection of avant-garde art in Paris, including Renoir's major canvas *Luncheon at Bougival* (Washington, the Phillips Collection) and one with a circus theme, *Jugglers at the Cirque Fernando* (Art Institute of Chicago). In fact, Princeteau took Lautrec to this popular circus on the boulevard Rochechouart at the foot of Montmartre, introducing him to the subject-matter for his later works.

Pierre Auguste Renoir, 1841-1919
Luncheon at Bougival, 1881
Canvas, 129.5 x 173 cm
Washington, the Phillips
Collection

Lautrec did not remain long with Princeteau, but transferred to the studio of Léon Bonnat (1833–1922) in April 1882. In a letter to his father on 17 April he wrote:

'I was received this morning by the students at Bonnat's studio. Thanks to the recommendations of Rachou, Ferréol's friend, I was given a good reception. By chance, a young American from the hotel started at the same time as me. We were made to talk and buy a drink. That was all. It wasn't so dreadful. There was a lot of noise, but little fighting. There are a lot of English and Americans.

'So that's me finally started. Draw, draw, that's the question. M. Moore, the deaf-mute American painter, brought in a lot of splendid Japanese curios.'

The choice of Bonnat's studio in the Impasse Hélène demonstrates how seriously Lautrec took his studies. It was a private atelier which took students who intended to compete for entry to the prestigious Ecole des Beaux-Arts. In the letter to his father quoted above Lautrec lays great emphasis on the drawing that students had to undertake at Bonnat's; even in the 1880s draughtsmanship was still regarded as forming the basis of all painting, in the traditional academic fashion. Typically students would study from plaster casts of antique sculpture and from the nude model for any figure painting. The work was demanding in these private studios, and students were expected to work on their own, contributing towards costs to cover heating, cleaning, the hire of the model and tuition, although often the master would make only brief weekly appearances. New students were expected to accept a degree of teasing, which could be forestalled, as Lautrec quickly learned, by buying the other students a drink.

The letter also records what may have been Lautrec's first encounter with the art of Japan, which had been popular in Paris with a small group of collectors since the 1860s and had been influential in many of the formal innovations of artists in the Impressionist circle, especially Degas. Increasingly, Lautrec was to adopt many of the oriental spatial conventions which he found in Japanese art, either directly or at second hand, through the influence of Degas, whose work he greatly admired at this time.

At first, however, his student works betray the lessons of the academic approach taught at Bonnat's. The loose handling and conventional pose of a painting such as *Seated Nude* of 1882 (see p. 15) demonstrate that this would not have been regarded as a finished painting but rather as an *étude*, a study, a work done in the studio from the life model which would have formed the basis for a more complex finished work.

After the summer spent in the south at Céleyran, Lautrec returned to Paris, where Bonnat closed his studio in September after his appointment as a professor at the Ecole des Beaux-Arts. Once again, a letter to the Comte seeks his approval for his new teacher:

'I've just taken a place at the studio of Cormon, a young and already famous painter, who did the celebrated *Cain Fleeing with his Family* which is in the Luxembourg. A powerful, austere and original talent ... Princeteau supports this choice. I should have liked to have tried Carolus, but the prince of colour turns out only mediocre draughtsmen, and that would have been fatal for me.'

First Communion Day, 1888
Cardboard, 63 x 36 cm
Toulouse, Musée des Augustins

The Laundress, 1889
Canvas, 93 x 75 cm
Paris, private collection

Already the academic reliance on the importance of drawing had infected Lautrec, and accounted for his not choosing to enter Carolus-Duran's atelier. Carolus-Duran (1838–1917) was one of the most fashionable portrait painters of the late nineteenth century, producing slick images with an almost photographic clarity. The studio of Fernand Cormon (1845–1924) one of the most remarkable teachers of the late nineteenth century, was in the boulevard de Clichy area of Montmartre. Emile Bernard, Louis Anquetin and Vincent Van Gogh all studied there, and Lautrec met each of them, as well as the artist René Grenier (1861–1917), with whom he lodged from 1884. A letter to his uncle, written on 1 December 1882, records that Cormon gave him a cordial welcome, and in particular admired his drawing. He continued, '... my new boss is the thinnest man in all of Paris. He comes to see us often, and wants us to amuse ourselves by painting outside the studio as frequently as possible'. Despite his teacher's praise for his drawing style, Lautrec seems to have resented his indulgence and to have missed the strict routine of Bonnat's. Nothing of the formal academic style of Cormon's *Cain* of 1880 (Paris, Musée d'Orsay), which was in the Luxembourg, the museum for contemporary art, seems to have had much effect on his students, and they seem to have been given a measure of freedom to develop an individual style. Under Cormon's tuition Lautrec's facility for drawing became more marked.

A contemporary photograph of Cormon's studio (see p.32) demonstrates the lighter side of life in the atelier when the master was absent. The conventional trappings of the studio are still there – the skeleton, the male nude model and the plaster casts in the background – but they have been joined by the studio dog. Toulouse-Lautrec is standing at the extreme left-hand side.

In 1884 Lautrec moved into the apartment of René and Lily Grenier in the rue Fontaine, which runs off the boulevard de Clichy. Around

Fernand Cormon, 1845-1924
Cain, 1880
Canvas, 384 x 700 cm
Paris, Musée d'Orsay

this time he stopped studying regularly at Cormon's, although he continued to drop in over the next few years, as much for the companionship the studio offered as for any tuition. His portrait *Emile Bernard* (see p. 22) demonstrates his fluency with a brush but its conventional treatment suggests he has yet to find a distinctive style. In his memoirs, Bernard (1868–1941) recounted that the work took twenty sittings before completion. In contrast, the portrait of *Vincent Van Gogh* (see p. 24), produced two years later, has been rapidly executed in pastel. Drawing on the colour combination of blue and yellow that Van Gogh (1853–1890) himself favoured, Lautrec has represented the sitter in a café with a solitary glass of absinthe. The long, loose strokes of the pastel capture the effects of light in a way that *Emile Bernard* fails to do. Pastel was a rare medium for Lautrec to use and one which may have been suggested to him by his admiration for Hilaire-Germain-Edgar Degas (1834–1917). He had probably met Degas in 1885, when he moved in with the Greniers, since the older artist had a studio in the same apartment block. The pattern made by the abstract shapes in the background suggests Degas' influence and the theme of the lonely figures in the café had been explored by him in *L'Absinthe* of 1876 (see p. 25).

By this time Lautrec had developed a personal style, drawing not only on Degas but on other artists for whom draughtsmanship was of primary importance, including Jean-Louis Forain (1852–1931) and Jean-François Raffaëlli (1850–1924), both of whom had exhibited with the Impressionists. Lautrec had never been attracted to the work of the landscape Impressionists, and even in early paintings of equestrian themes such as *At Chantilly Races* (see p. 10) the landscape functions merely as a backdrop rather than as an opportunity to study the effects of light in the open air. Like the circle of artists who worked around Degas, Lautrec was interested in the human figure and a work such as *First Communion Day* (see p. 28) draws on an almost caricatural social observance, taking in the unaccustomed formal clothing of the family as they proudly step out in the Paris streets. This work originally appeared in *Paris Illustré*, edited by his friend Maurice Joyant, and formed the illustration for a series of articles about the city, entitled 'L'Eté à Paris'.

In Cormon's studio

The Trace-Horse of the Omnibus Company, 1888
Cardboard, 80 x 51 cm
Paris, private collection

Juliette Vary, 1888

Juliette V., Model in the Studio,
1888
Cardboard, 75 x 50 cm
Bremen, Kunsthalle

36

Chapter 2

Montmartre and Aristide Bruant

In the 1880s Montmartre, where Lautrec lived and worked, still retained the rural character which set it apart from Paris proper. It had only recently been united with the capital, just before the Franco-Prussian War of 1870. Although the hill of the Butte Montmartre was surrounded by large boulevards with heavy traffic at its base, the centre was still like a village, with windmills and livestock in small fields. During the Commune, Montmartre had opposed the government forces and it was still regarded as a centre of radical politics. The craftspeople, traditional inhabitants of the area, had recently been joined by anarchists and bourgeois artists, who favoured the Batignolles quarter. The area's prostitutes were as likely to be ordinary streetwalkers as women who worked in the ostentatious brothels and places of popular entertainment flourishing on the boulevards.

By the end of the century Paris had 27,000 cafés, and in the era before the rise in the cinema they were the focus of a genuinely popular culture, helping to create a sense of local and class identity. They were particularly significant in a large city, where much of the workforce comprised rootless immigrants from the provinces. Used by the working classes, these places provided warmth, company and the escape offered by alcohol, and their clientele spread to the bourgeois and bohemian inhabitants of the area. Government restrictions on the use of theatrical costume in unlicensed theatres had been relaxed in 1865, giving rise to the informal café-concert, which provided a democratic alternative to the theatre. The entertainment provided was often secondary to the food, drink and audience participation which these places offered. Much cheaper than their upper-class counterparts, they had the added advantage that one did not have to dress formally to attend.

The development of Montmartre as an area of popular amusement was largely due to the enterprising nature of a former artist, Rodolphe Salis, who had opened a cabaret, Le Chat Noir, in his studio on the boulevard Rochechouart. In 1885 he sold up to one of the performers, Aristide Bruant (1851–1925). Bruant changed its name to Le Mirliton, which means 'the toy flute', an allusion to the kind of popular music that was enjoyed there. Lautrec had begun frequenting cabarets with Princeteau and became a regular at Bruant's establishment, probably through the introduction of Anquetin, which was promoted as 'the place to visit if you want to be insulted'.

After working as a jeweller and as an employee with the Chemins de Fer de la Compagnie du Nord, Bruant began singing in cafés in his spare time, transforming popular jokes into songs which relied for their impact on the richness of working-class urban slang and humour. Capitalising on the gulf between high and low culture, Bruant mocked the élitism of the theatre and its audience by treating

A Batignolles, 1888
Canvas, 92 x 65 cm
London, private collection

Justine Dieuhl, 1891. Cardboard, 75 x 58 cm. Paris, Musée d'Orsay

Aristide Bruant

everyone at his cabaret as democratically as possible, uniformly insulting them all, both individually and collectively. This cavalier approach made him the darling of popular entertainment, and his audiences comprised the bourgeoisie and the local artisans alike.

The aristocratic writer Edmond de Goncourt described the 'vulgar abuse' hurled by the *chanson-cabaretier* at a polite gathering in 1892, not without a certain *frisson*:

'He appeared wearing a blood-red shirt, with a velvet jacket and long polished leather gaiters ... [He] produces an overall impression of an enigmatic androgyne.

'What he sang before the society women who were there was quite indescribable. This ignoble lyricism consisted of foul adjectives, dirty words, purulent slang, the vocabulary of sordid brothels and clinics for venereal diseases.

'You have to see Bruant belching this out in his brassy voice, see him as I saw him ... meanwhile I, for all that I am no prude, had the impression that I was attending a prison concert ... and to think that those society women, without the protection of a fan, without even a blush on their cheeks ... smiled and clapped their

Woman with Red Hair in the
Garden of Père Forest, 1889
Canvas, 75 x 60 cm
New York, private collection

Red Haired Woman seen from behind, 1891
Cardboard, 78 x 59.7 cm
Albi, Musée Toulouse-Lautrec

pretty aristocratic hands at words no different from the obscene scribblings on walls from which they avert their eyes.'

He concluded prophetically: 'Oh, Bruant's songs in society drawing-rooms and dynamite in carriage entrances! These are two warning signs of the approaching end of the bourgeois age'. It was, of course, essential to his beliefs that Bruant was an anarchist and de Goncourt quite rightly saw his act as part of a larger attempt at affronting bourgeois sensibilities, linking it with recent politically motivated bombings.

During the show Bruant sold copies of *Le Mirliton* for ten centimes. This was a newspaper which he edited and for which Lautrec produced several illustrations. In the edition that appeared on 29 December 1885 Lautrec produced a photorelief, and in total he illustrated four covers of the magazine, three of them laboriously stencilled from separate plates. It was through his friendship with Bruant that Lautrec gained entry to the bohemian underworld of Montmartre.

Woman with a Black Feather Boa, c.1892
Cardboard, 53 x 41 cm
Paris, Musée d'Orsay

Georges Seurat, 1859–1891
Un Dimanche à la Grande-Jatte, 1886
Canvas, 206 x 306 cm
The Art Institute of Chicago, Helen Birch Bartlett Memorial Collection

1886

The eighth and final Impressionist exhibition was held from 15 May to 15 June 1886 and is often regarded as signifying the end of an era in avant-garde painting. The original group of painters who had exhibited together had long since broken up, either for ideological, aesthetic or personal reasons. Monet and Renoir had both reverted to sending their works to the Salon, the state-supported annual exhibition to which the Impressionists had initially been so opposed. Renoir had acknowledged the frankly financial motivation of his defection, writing to his dealer in 1881 that '... there are scarcely 15 collectors in Paris capable of admiring a painter without the Salon. There are 80,000 of them who won't buy as much as a nose if the artist hasn't been shown at the Salon'. Later the same year he had visited Italy where he had admired the works of the Renaissance; this led him to reassess his working practice in the light of the old masters and to adopt the characteristic 'dry' style of the mid-1880s epitomised by the *Bathers* of 1887 (Philadelphia Museum of Art), in which the role of line and the conventional grouping of the large studio painting is far from the informal landscapes of his high Impressionist period.

In fact, little pure landscape painting remained at the final Impressionist show. Degas had established a band of protégés at the exhibition, including Forain and Mary Cassatt, whose chief interests lay in the depiction of the human figure indoors. Landscape Impressionists such as Camille Pissarro showed several works which

The Policeman's Daughter, 1890
Cardboard, 67 x 50 cm
Hamburg, Kunsthalle

were influenced by the divisionist technique of Georges Seurat, whose large *Un Dimanche à la Grande-Jatte* of 1886 (Art Institute of Chicago) (see p. 43) marked both a consolidation of and a departure from traditional Impressionist practice. The study of the effects of light and atmosphere which had concerned the landscape Impressionists is here taken to its logical conclusion, resulting in a carefully contrived, artfully painted, massive studio work which runs contrary to the ethos of the informality of the Impressionist sketch. The work of Paul Gauguin, who had been exhibiting with the Impressionists for several years, was still impressionistic in handling and subject-matter, but later that year he was to produce a number of works in Brittany which were to depart radically from his earlier practice.

By 1886 Lautrec was no longer attending Cormon's atelier except on an informal basis, but he met Vincent Van Gogh there after the Dutchman's arrival in Paris in February of that year. By this time, Lautrec had developed a personal style which in fact owed little to any of the artists working around him – certainly not to his three teachers nor to the Impressionist artists (although he had visited Monet in 1885), nor to the younger artists working at Cormon's with whose work he came into regular contact.

The most lasting impact seems to have come from the work of Degas, and a painting such as *The Laundress* of 1889 (see p. 30) owes much to his example. The theme of working-class women was a popular one, not only with painters such as Degas and Bonvin; it was also taken up by naturalist writers such as Zola, most notably in *L'Assommoir*, which had been published in 1877. Like Degas, Lautrec has depicted his model within a dark and claustrophobic interior, ironically looking out onto the rooftops of Paris. He has turned her away from the viewer, and has further obscured her face by letting her hair fall over it. Any suggestion of the personality of the woman therefore rests on what he can convey by her gesture and position, which emphasise the gruelling and repetitive nature of her work. Her relative anonymity further conveys a deep sense of alienation: laundresses were often immigrants from the provinces who had to supplement their income with prostitution or part-time modelling. The model for this work has been identified as Carmen Gaudin, whom Toulouse-Lautrec often used at this time – apparently on account of her red hair which he particularly admired. The work was reproduced in *Paris Illustré* in July 1888.

The other main artistic influence on Lautrec in Paris was the art of Japan; works by the masters of *ukiyo-e* had been collected in France from the 1860s. Samuel Bing (1838–1905), an art dealer from Hamburg who had arrived in Paris in 1871, had travelled in the Far East in 1875. Edmond de Goncourt had visited his shop in 1877 and noted that it specialised in 'Japanese curios'. Lautrec certainly bought from Bing and also from Portier in the rue Lepic, who lived in the same apartment block as the Van Gogh brothers. His personal collection of Japanese prints dates from 1883 when he saw an exhibition in Georges Petit's gallery.

A work such as *The Trace-Horse of the Omnibus Company* of 1888 (see p. 33) demonstrates how Lautrec appropriated certain Japanese devices for his own ends. The work was published in the

Poudre de Riz, 1887-1888
Cardboard, 56 x 46 cm
Amsterdam, Vincent Van Gogh
Foundation,
Rijksmuseum Vincent Van Gogh

46

Edouard Manet, 1832-1883
Nana, 1877
Canvas, 150 x 116 cm
Hamburg, Kunsthalle

Paris Illustré of 7 July 1888 along with *First Communion Day* (see p. 28) to illustrate Emile Michelet's article 'L'Eté à Paris'. Lautrec has borrowed the rushing diagonal lines of the Japanese print-makers, the unusual viewpoint of the horse, the suppression of shadows, the decorative arabesques and the abrupt cutting off of the omnibus at the left-hand side. Other distinctive Japanese features, such as the broad washes of flat colour, were properly to be used only when he started making lithographs.

By 1886 Lautrec had formed a distinctive style; he had begun to exhibit works on a permanent basis at Le Mirliton, with whose patron he had become friendly; and had he taken a studio on his own in the rue Caulaincourt in the centre of Montmartre.

Models

One favourite model at this time, Juliette Vary, sometimes wrongly identified as Hélène Vary, was depicted by Lautrec in 1888 (see p. 34). She had been a professional model since childhood and

Pierre Auguste Renoir, 1841-1919
*The Ball at the Moulin de la
Galette,* 1876
Canvas, 131 x 175 cm
Paris, Musée d'Orsay

Dance at the Moulin de la Galette, 1889
Canvas, 88.5 x 101.3 cm
The Art Institute of Chicago,
Mr and Mrs Lewis Larned Coburn
Memorial Collection

At the Cirque Fernando: The Equestrienne, 1888
Canvas, 100.3 x 161.3 cm
The Art Institute of Chicago,
The Joseph Winterbotham
Collection

the work derives from a contemporary photograph of her which shows her in the same strongly profiled pose. It is difficult to say exactly what the status of the painting is – neither is it properly a genre scene like *The Laundress*, nor is it a study of a female model which could be used to form the basis of a finished painting, like *Seated Nude* (see p. 15), nor is it a naturalistic study – the stark line of her profile betrays Lautrec's reliance on the photograph. Instead, he seems to have been attempting to confect a vision of the artist's studio – with several large canvases stacked against the back wall and a demurely dressed young woman sitting in a chair with a newspaper on her lap – which accords with the vision he outlined to his mother when he wrote to her in the summer of 1888: 'What's new? No doubt more is happening for you than for me, as I am leading a dull life. If I didn't have the showers and my work, I should be bored to death ...'

Edgar Degas, 1834-1917
*Miss Lala at the Cirque
Fernando,* 1879
Canvas, 117 x 77.5 cm
London, National Gallery

52

Mlle Dihau at the Piano, 1890
Canvas, 68 x 48.5 cm
Albi, Musée Toulouse-Lautrec

A Batignolles (see p. 36), painted at about the same time, and depicting a red-haired woman standing against a backdrop of foliage, was intended as an illustration for one of Bruant's popular songs that had the same title, about different areas of the capital. The painting had the following lines from the ballad attached to it:

'Quand on s'balladait sous le ciel bleu
Avec ses ch'veux couleur de feu
On croyait voir eun'aureole
A Batignolles.'

The following year Lautrec returned to the same motif of a young woman pictured against a screen of greenery in *Woman with Red Hair in the Garden of Père Forest* (see p. 40). This was one of a number of similar portraits that the artist produced between 1888 and 1891 depicting women in the overrun garden of Père Forest on the corner of the rue Caulaincourt, where he had his studio, and the boulevard de Clichy. Playing on the complementary colours green and red, the landscape continues to function merely as a backdrop to the figure, and is reduced to a largely decorative role. *Justine Dieuhl* of 1891 (see p. 38) belongs to the same series. As with *Woman with Red Hair in the Garden of Père Forest*, Lautrec has depicted his model from a much closer range than was recommended for portraiture, closing in on the young woman to such an extent that he is simultaneously looking into her eyes and down onto her clasped hands. This would suggest that the painting was largely finished away from the motif: the practicalities of erecting his easel this close to the subject and working from life would have made such a viewpoint virtually impossible.

The fluency of a work such as *Woman with a Black Feather Boa* of c. 1892 (see p. 42) is in marked contrast to the rather more studied portraits of female sitters such as *The Policeman's Daughter* of 1890 (see p. 44), which depicts Bruant's sister-in-law. In the former, painted in oil on cardboard, he has used the colour of his support throughout the work not only to provide the rich ochre of the background but also to enliven the otherwise cool tonalities of the face and clothing. The work uses a minimum of colours, which facilitates a rapid execution, and may have been derived from his practice in print-making. Lautrec's satisfaction with the work is evident from the fact that he included it in an exhibition of his works in London in 1898.

Les XX

In 1887 Lautrec rented an apartment with Dr Henri Bourges at 19 rue Fontaine, running off the boulevard de Clichy. That same year he met the Belgian artist Théo Van Rysselberghe (1862–1926), who invited him to exhibit with Les XX the following February in Brussels. Les XX (The Twenty) had been formed in 1883 by twenty Belgian artists and a lawyer, Octave Maus, largely to provide an alternative exhibition space for artists who had been refused entry by the jury of the official Salon in Brussels. From the outset their intention was to be at the vanguard of European art, and their constitution allowed invited artists to submit works to be hung along-

side those by members of the group. Their first exhibition was held in 1884 and the works of artists such as Van Rysselberghe and James Ensor (1860–1949) were displayed with those of guests such as Whistler, Sargent and Rodin. Annual exhibitions were held until 1893, when the society was voluntarily disbanded, to be reformed with the wider purpose of including design as well as 'high' art under the new name of La Libre Esthétique. Renoir and Monet were guests in 1886 and Pissarro and Seurat in 1887, evidence that Les XX watched Paris closely for examples of innovative art.

Toulouse-Lautrec participated in the fifth annual exhibition in 1888, to which Anquetin and the Divisionist painters Paul Signac (1863–1935) and Albert Dubois-Pillet (1846–1890) were also invited. He exhibited one drawing and eleven paintings, including *Poudre de Riz* of 1887–1888 (see p. 46). The work appears Divisionist: colours have not been mixed on the palette, but rather their constituent pigments have been juxtaposed on the canvas, using the characteristic 'pointillist' brushstroke, with the desired effect that they are mixed optically, thereby enhancing their luminosity. This method of working was popular at this time among avant-garde circles: Pissarro and Seurat had both exhibited Divisionist works at the final Impressionist exhibition in 1886; Dubois-Pillet and Signac had been invited to Brussels; and even Van Gogh, working in Paris, had attempted the technique in *Interior of a Restaurant* (Otterlo, Rijksmuseum Kröller-Müller), painted between April and June 1887. Lautrec has not systematised his brushstroke in quite the same way as Van Gogh or any of the other artists. It is rather a refinement of the flickering Impressionist facture than a regular dot but its use achieves a fusion of foreground and background in a manner that is quite different from contemporary works such as *A Batignolles* (see p. 36).

The model for *Poudre de Riz* was Marie-Clémentine – known as Suzanne – Valadon (1865–1938), whom Lautrec had met in 1885 and who became his lover at this time. After a career in the circus, cut short by an accident, she became a professional model and later a painter in her own right. The work takes its title from the tin of face powder on the table in front of the model, although just where she is supposed to be sitting is not made clear. There is no mirror in front of her and instead she gazes impassively at the spectator. The work continues a favourite theme in late nineteenth century French art – that of applying cosmetics. Baudelaire, in his *Painter of Modern Life*, had lauded the use of make-up, and the analogy between the contrived 'natural' beauty of the woman and the artist's role as a creator was there to be drawn. Manet's painting *Nana* of 1877 (see p. 47) shows a demi-mondaine at her toilet, glancing seductively at the viewer, and Seurat produced the painting *Young Woman Powdering Herself* (London, Courtauld Institute Galleries), which was begun in 1888. In both of these works, however, the woman is depicted at a mirror, and in the guise of a flirt. The world-weary nature of the model in *Poudre de Riz*, the absence of any mirror, and her calculating stare at the spectator, mean that the work can be read as a comment on the transitory nature of beauty and of art.

Henri Samary at the Comédie Française, 1889
Cardboard, 75 x 52 cm
Paris, Musée d'Orsay

The Dance at the Moulin Rouge, 1890
Canvas, 115 x 150 cm
Philadelphia Museum of Art,
The Henry P.McIlhenny Collection

Lautrec painting *The Dance at the Moulin Rouge*

At the Moulin Rouge, 1892
Canvas, 123 x 141 cm
The Art Institute of Chicago
Helen Birch Bartlett Memorial
Collection

Lautrec with Tremolada
admiring Chéret's
poster for the Moulin Rouge

Chapter 3

1889 – the Exposition Universelle

In 1889 France staged an Exposition Universelle, to celebrate the centennial of the French Revolution. These international exhibitions had been introduced under Napoleon III but that of 1889 was the most lavish yet. It was intended to demonstrate the French Republic's commercial, colonial and cultural pre-eminence to the rest of the world. The newly erected Eiffel Tower was a symbol of national pride and dominated the exhibition site. A number of art exhibitions were held and a large part of the display at the Salon was intended to serve as a gathering of native French talent, so it included works by Manet, who had died in 1883, and Cézanne, who had never been previously accepted by a Salon jury.

Of course, there were a number of alternative venues. There, the work on display was quite different from that validated by the French State, and was representative of the work of the younger generation of avant-garde artists. In the summer of 1889 Gauguin, Anquetin and Bernard exhibited with other artists at the Café Volpini, in the so-called 'Groupe impressionniste et synthétiste', the aims of which were closely allied to those of the Symbolist poets and opposed to the naturalism that they felt had characterised Impressionism and the work of writers such as Zola. Lautrec exhibited at the Cercle Artistique et Littéraire Volney in June, and in September to October at the fourth Salon des Indépendants, with Van Gogh, Anquetin, Seurat and Signac. At this prestigious show he exhibited *Dance at the Moulin de la Galette* of 1889 (see p. 48), with which he must have been pleased since he also sent it to the exhibition of Les XX in 1890. This was Lautrec's first picture of a dance-hall. It marked an important departure in his art, away from the social commentary of works such as *The Laundress* (see p. 30) and *First Communion Day* (see p. 28), towards a subject-matter with which he is now for ever inextricably linked, suggesting as it does a kind of escapism and *fin-de-siècle* decadence. The contrast between the earlier works and the kind of hedonism found in these multi-figure compositions is very marked.

The Moulin de la Galette stood at the top of the Butte Montmartre, and had been the subject of a major canvas by Renoir in 1876, *The Ball at the Moulin de la Galette* (see p. 49). Situated in a windmill, and with a yard at the back for dancing out of doors, it was quite different in character from the more ostentatious establishments on the boulevards. It retained its rural character and was largely frequented by the working classes, although artists would sometimes climb up the hillside to it on a Sunday afternoon.

Drawing on the influence of Japanese prints, especially in his depiction of space, Lautrec has produced a work which is partly an academic exercise, partly an Impressionistic representation of a scene. The split between the four foreground figures, each carefully contrived from a variety of angles, and the background mass

At the Moulin Rouge: La Goulue,
1891
Poster, 195 x 122 cm

Aristide Bruant at Les Ambassadeurs, 1892
Paper, mounted on canvas,
255 x 120 cm
Albi, Musée Toulouse-Lautrec

The Englishman at the Moulin Rouge, 1892
Cardboard, 57.3 x 45.3 cm
Albi, Musée Toulouse-Lautrec

means that the reliance on the rushing diagonals of the backs of the seats at the edge of the dance-hall to suggest space is particularly evident. The device of the empty table in the foreground, which suggests a means of entry into the picture space for the spectator, was one which had been used by Degas, most notably in his *L'Absinthe* of 1876 (see p. 25). The themes of the cabaret and the popular dance-hall were to become increasingly important for Lautrec. He switched his allegiance away from the Moulin de la Galette towards the Moulin Rouge when it opened in 1889 on the boulevard de Clichy to cater for the crowds who flocked to Paris to attend the Exposition Universelle.

The Cirque Fernando

In 1888 Lautrec had produced his first major circus painting, *At the Cirque Fernando: the Equestrienne* (see p. 50), which he sent to the exhibition of Les XX that year, demonstrating the importance that he attached to it. Over five feet long, it was a major representation of a theme to which he would return on several occasions over the next few years.

Aristide Bruant on his Bicycle, 1892
Cardboard, 74.5 x 65 cm
Albi, Musée Toulouse-Lautrec

Aristide Bruant, 1893
Poster without imprint,
127 x 92.5 cm

The Cirque Fernando, on the corner of the rue des Martyrs and the boulevard Rochechouart, was just along from Le Mirliton, which Lautrec frequented at this time. Both Degas and Renoir had painted there in the 1870s, and Degas' *Miss Lala at the Cirque Fernando* (see p. 51) had been shown at the fourth Impressionist exhibition of 1879; Renoir's *Jugglers at the Cirque Fernando* (Art Institute of Chicago), painted in 1879, was included in the seventh show in 1882.

Both Impressionist painters had exploited the theatrical elements of the circus: the effects of artificial lighting on the performers' clothing; the lines of the building itself and the unnatural poses which the performers adopted in the course of their acts. *At the Cirque Fernando: The Equestrienne* builds on that tradition, but goes further in its treatment of space, arching the ring round behind the performers, and flattening their bodies, in a radical departure from the norms of Western perspective. The influence of Japanese art is particularly evident here, not only in the push towards a two-dimensionality but in the flat colours and the bleached ground with

*Jane Avril leaving the Moulin
Rouge,* 1892
Cardboard, 84.4 x 63.5 cm
Hartford, Wadsworth Atheneum,
Bequest of George A. Gay

*Jane Avril in the Entrance of the
Moulin Rouge,* 1892
Cardboard, 103 x 55 cm
London, Courtauld Institute
Galleries

Jane Avril Dancing, c.1892
Cardboard, 85.5 x 45 cm
Paris, Musée d'Orsay

Jane Avril Dancing, 1893
Canvas, 101 x 75 cm
Paris, private collection

its total absence of shadows. The suggestion of movement which had interested Lautrec at the outset of his career in paintings such as *At Chantilly Races* (see p. 10) is treated very differently here. In the early works it was suggested by a fluent painterly handling but in this picture it is conveyed by the grossly foreshortened horse and the sweep of the circus ring.

The female horsewoman had been modelled by Suzanne Valadon, who had also sat for *Poudre de Riz* (see p. 46) at this time, which was also included in Lautrec's début at Les XX. If *Poudre de Riz* pointed the way backwards in terms of its still Impressionistic handling and its introspective theme, *At the Cirque Fernando: The Equestrienne* marked the inception of a radical departure in terms of handling, treatment of space and particularly in its subject-matter.

The painting was bought by Oller and Zidler, the proprietors of the Moulin Rouge, and it hung in the foyer there where it was particularly admired by Seurat whose last major painting *The Circus* (Paris, Musée d'Orsay), left unfinished at the time of his death in

Divan Japonais, 1892
Poster, 80 x 60 cm

1891, uses the same subject of the female bare-back rider and a similarly radical flattening of the picture space.

At this time Lautrec painted intimate scenes of young female models such as *Mlle Dihau at the Piano* of 1890 (see p. 52), continuing the depiction of introspective domestic scenes begun in the earlier portraits of his mother which were to reach their conclusion in the works he produced in the *maisons closes*, such as *In Bed* (see p. 132) and *Woman at her Toilet: Mme Poupoule* (see p. 154). Representations of men tended to be quite different, the portrait of the actor *Henri Samary at the Comédie Française* of 1889 (see p. 54) depicts him in the role of Raoul de Vaubert from the comedy by Jules Sandeau. He is shown full-length against a background of painted scenery, and his ostentatious extrovert performance is quite markedly different from that of the bourgeois woman in the claustrophobic interior. It is really only in Lautrec's representations of women in the dance-halls or the cabarets that they enter properly into the public domain, and are allowed full expression of their personalities.

Jane Avril, 1899
Poster, 56 x 36 cm

Chapter 4

The Moulin Rouge

The Moulin Rouge was opened on 15 October 1889 in the place Blanche, at number 90 boulevard de Clichy, just along from Cormon's Montmartre studio. This popular dance-hall and *café chantant* was the brainchild of the Spanish impresario Joseph Oller (1839–1922), who founded a number of other clubs in Paris, including Le Nouveau Cirque and Le Jardin de Paris. Its entrance on the boulevard was through a large replica windmill, decorated with stars and a crescent moon suspended on wires. Behind this was a large ballroom surrounded by a gallery lined with tables. Every Wednesday and Saturday evening a ball would be held there and on fine evenings the dancers and orchestra would move out into the tree-lined garden at the back of the building. This was decorated with a large elephant inherited from one of the sites at the Exposition Universelle. Posters and paintings, including Lautrec's *At the Cirque Fernando: The Equestrienne* (see p. 50) were displayed in the foyer. As at the other Montmartre venues, the clientele was mixed, but for some time the Moulin Rouge was popular with aristocratic figures.

Lautrec worked at the Moulin Rouge until 1896, producing some thirty images of it, including *The Dance at the Moulin Rouge* of 1890 (see p. 56). This work continues the themes established in *Dance at the Moulin de la Galette* (see p. 48) painted the previous year, with sharply focused foreground figures and hazier background elements. Here, however, the attention is centred on the two dancers in the middle of the work – a woman performing the so-called *quadrille naturaliste*, a revival of the can-can, and her male partner Valentin le Désossé (1843–1907). Several of the figures in the background are identifiable, including the photographer Paul Sescau, Maurice Guibert, François Gauzi and the artist Marcellin Desboutin. The profile of the woman in the foreground is sometimes said to represent Jane Avril. The work is in effect a group portrait of Lautrec's acquaintances and is therefore similar to works by Manet, such as *Music in the Tuileries Gardens* (London, National Gallery) which also represents a popular place of bourgeois leisure. In their informal groupings and the use each makes of the radical cutting-off of figures to the edges of the canvas, both works attempt an evocation of fashionable urban life.

Two years later Lautrec produced *At the Moulin Rouge* (see p. 58). Formally, it is much closer to *Dance at the Moulin de la Galette*, with the emphasis placed on the diagonal of the balustrade in the foreground, which serves simultaneously to involve and distance the spectator in the scene. Once again, the work is a cunningly contrived group portrait rather than a scene of reportage. The bearded figure to the left-hand side is the Symbolist critic Edouard Dujardin; Sescau and Guibert are present again, as well as La Macarona, a Spanish dancer who worked at the Moulin Rouge. In the background the entertainer La Goulue is shown rearranging

La Goulue entering the Moulin Rouge, 1892
Cardboard, 79.4 x 59 cm
New York, Museum of Modern Art, Gift of Mrs David M.Levy

Paul Signac, 1863-1935
Félix Fénéon, 1890
Canvas, 74 x 95 cm
New York, Museum of
Modern Art,
Collection Joshua Logan

her hair, and the artist himself glides past, accompanied by the tall figure of his cousin Dr Gabriel Tapié de Céleyran (1869–1930), who had arrived in Paris to practise medicine the previous year and with whom Lautrec continued to be intimate until his death. The woman in the foreground, her face garishly illuminated by the artificial lighting, was identified as Miss Nelly C. Her proximity to the viewer is simultaneously denied by the thick lines which outline her costume and attach her firmly to the figures in the middle distance. Once again, the treatment of space is influenced by oriental example. The crisply delineated foreground figures are contrasted with blurred background elements, and the lights which were evident in *The Dance at the Moulin Rouge* are treated in an almost abstract way. In both these paintings the limited palette and contrast of sharp clear colours, derived from the effects of artificial lighting, point the way towards the clarity and economy of Lautrec's poster design.

Preparing for the Quadrille, 1892
Cardboard, 80.1 x 60.5 cm
Washington, National Gallery
of Art,
Chester Dale Collection

Posters

By 1891 the Moulin Rouge had declined in popularity, and the fashionable customers had moved on. In an attempt to attract them back, the proprietor Zidler made several improvements. He lured

La Goulue Dancing, 1895
(Panel for La Goulue's Booth at
the Foire du Trône)
Canvas, 285 x 307.5 cm
Paris, Musée d'Orsay

La Goulue

*La Goulue Dancing with Valentin
le Désossé,* 1895
(Panel for La Goulue's Booth at
the Foire du Trône)
Canvas, 298 x 316 cm
Paris, Musée d'Orsay

*Yvette Guilbert taking a Curtain
Call*, 1894
Paper, 48 x 28 cm
Albi, Musée Toulouse-Lautrec

Yvette Guilbert, 1894
Paper, 186 x 92 cm
Albi, Musée Toulouse-Lautrec

Mlle Yvette Guilbert

Yvette Guilbert's Black Gloves,
1894
Cardboard, 62.8 x 37 cm
Albi, Musée Toulouse-Lautrec

a number of celebrated entertainers to work for him, including La Goulue, who was then at the peak of her success and could earn 3,750 francs a week. Toulouse-Lautrec was commissioned to provide a poster advertising the re-opened Moulin Rouge, and its fresh design was chosen because of its modern associations. A contemporary photograph (see p. 59) shows Zidler's assistant Trémolada standing beside Lautrec, admiring the original poster advertising the Moulin Rouge. This had been commissioned in 1889 from the famous poster artist Jules Chéret (1836–1932).

Chéret had worked in England from 1859 to 1866, studying mechanical printing processes, and had produced posters for the

Mlle Marcelle Lender, 1895
Lithograph, 37 x 28 cm

perfumer Rimmel. In France he was responsible for popularising the poster as a respectable art form. Although posters had been used for commercial purposes in Paris since the end of the eighteenth century, these had been small and with the emphasis on the text. It was only recently that the improvement in graphic processes had led to their development. Chéret popularised the use of the mechanical rather than the hand press, making large print runs much easier and cheaper and posters more widely available, and allowing for much larger works to be produced. Until the middle of the nineteenth century posters were printed on small white sheets in black ink. It was Chéret who first concentrated attention on the image rather than the text, making the coloured shapes much more accessible and instantly recognisable across a busy city street. He too dispensed with illusionistic conventions inherited from the high art tradition, including shading and traditional Western depiction of space. Instead his bold, direct works emphasise their two-dimensionality. In the photograph Trémolada points to the merits of Chéret's design and Lautrec has taken the unusual step of removing his hat, presumably in mock deference to the master. However,

Marcelle Lender dancing the Bolero in 'Chilpéric', c. 1895
Canvas, 145 x 150 cm
New York, Collection Mr and Mrs
John Hay Whitney

Miss May Belfort taking a Bow,
1895
Lithograph, 37.2 x 26.5 cm
Albi, Musée Toulouse-Lautrec

May Belfort, 1895
Poster, 80 x 60 cm
Albi, Musée Toulouse-Lautrec

Miss May Belfort, 1895
Canvas, 63 x 48.5 cm
Cleveland Museum of Art

the work's fussiness and attention to detail meant that it had ceased
to function properly as an advertisement for the Moulin Rouge,
and Lautrec was faced with the practical problem of finding an even
more arresting and evocative image to popularise the place.

At the Moulin Rouge: La Goulue (see p. 61) was Lautrec's first
attempt at a print, and the strong, simplified shapes and easily recognisable product made it an unqualified success. In October, he wrote
to his mother how much he had enjoyed making the poster and
the feeling of authority over the printer's studio. 'My poster is
stuck on the walls of Paris today, and I'm going to do another one.'

The poster depicts the famous dancer Louise Weber (1870–1929),
nicknamed La Goulue (The Glutton), the star attraction of the
revamped dance-hall, sandwiched between the dark silhouettes of
the top-hatted onlookers in the background and the grey foreground
figure of her dancing partner, Etienne Renaudin (1843–1907), known
as Valentin le Désossé (The Boneless One). This famous dancing
team had made their professional début at the Moulin de la Galette,
exploiting the contrast between the ungainly movements of Désossé

Mlle Polaire, 1895
Cardboard, 56 x 41 cm
Albi, Musée Toulouse-Lautrec

and the erotic display of La Goulue's high-kicking style. The poster is a refinement of earlier paintings, particularly *The Dance at the Moulin Rouge* (see p. 56), which had also featured Désossé. In both, the background figures provide a screen and the foreground silhouette a counterpoise to the real action in the middle distance. The feature of the lights is here reduced to simple yellow shapes floating over the heads of the onlookers and balanced by the mass of lights in the foreground. Lautrec has borrowed Chéret's sinuous line but has greatly simplified the image, removing any superficial prettiness. The emphasis is on flat washes of colour but in the foreground figure of Désossé Lautrec has used a special technique which involved spraying inks through a sieve with a brush, leading to a much more delicately nuanced tone with red, blue and black inks superimposed. The poster had a print run of between one and three thousand, and its display across Paris in October 1891 made Lautrec immediately popular. That he regarded the work highly is evident from the fact that he included it with the works he sent for exhibition with Les XX in Brussels in February 1892. From 1891 until his death ten years later, he produced a further 350 lithographs, 30 of which were posters.

Oscar Wilde, 1895
Cardboard, 60 x 50 cm
Private collection

At 'La Mie', 1891
Cardboard, 53 x 67.8 cm
Boston, Museum of Fine Arts,
S.A. Denio Collection and General
Income

Gabriel Tapié de Céleyran, 1894
Canvas, 110 x 56 cm
Albi, Musée Toulouse-Lautrec

Lithography

The immediate popularity of *At the Moulin Rouge: La Goulue* was part of a growing interest in lithography in France at this time. Monochrome lithography had been discovered accidentally in Germany by Aloys Senefelder (1771–1834) in 1797, but had not become popular in France until the 1820s. Major practitioners included Géricault, Delacroix and particularly Daumier, who exploited its democratic associations for his satirical and political prints. Lithography is based on the chemical principle that grease repels water. The artist draws a design onto a porous lithographic stone, using a fatty chalk crayon. (This process later became more sophisticated and a brush loaded with a greasy ink was substituted for the crayon, lending a much greater freedom to the handling. Similarly, the original limestone was often replaced by a zinc plate.) This design is fixed onto the stone or zinc surface by the printer, using an increasingly sophisticated cocktail of chemicals. The porous stone is then saturated with water, and the fatty areas repel the

Au Moulin Rouge: La Goulue and la Môme Fromage, 1892
One of the first colour lithographs by Lautrec, 45.8 x 34.7 cm

Sarah Bernhardt in 'Phèdre', 1893
Lithograph, 32.5 x 23.5 cm

moisture. Next, the entire surface is spread with the same greasy ink used for the drawing, and the moistened areas act as a repellant. A sheet of paper is pressed onto the stone and the whole thing is passed through a lithographic press. Originally this was operated by hand but with advances in technology a steam-driven press was used, making the work less laborious and quicker. Of course, different stones had to be used for the different colours and each had to be drawn individually. For *At the Moulin Rouge: La Goulue* Lautrec used three stones, one for each of the black, yellow and red colours.

Lithography was the first new method of print-making since the fifteenth century and was frequently seen as being more democratic than the 'high' art print media, such as engraving or etching. This was partly because the practice depended on the role of the printer, making it a much more craft-oriented activity than a process such as etching which the artist controls from beginning to end. The use of limestone allowed larger images to be produced and their

Cléo de Mérode, c.1895
Lithograph, 29.5 x 24.1 cm

bold handling was quite different from the tight technique used in engraving and etching. In addition, lithography was much more populist in its orientation. Satirical journals and newspapers often used lithographs for illustration and the ephemeral poster was the quintessential art of the streets, as Toulouse-Lautrec rightly recognised from the outset. It offered a far greater variety of effects than the other print media: the design could be drawn on with a crayon or washed on with a brush, which allowed for an increased freedom of execution. The greasy ink could be applied thickly or thinly, in opaque or transparent washes, and a variety of textures could be achieved. Lautrec was one of the first to use the Japanese method of spattering the stone with a brush through a sieve, a technique known as *crachis*. The formal advances which he had already

Cipa Godebski, 1896
Cardboard, 52 x 40 cm
Paris, private collection

96

begun to make in his paintings before 1891, particularly those representing dance-hall scenes, were only properly exploited in the medium of the lithograph, with its emphasis on broadly simplified forms, large areas of unmodelled colour and the suppression of any Western spatial conventions.

The traditional hierarchy of subject-matter and media which had been established and controlled by the Académie Française since the seventeenth century was being eroded by the 1890s, and this contributed to the interest in posters and lithographs, which previously had been perceived as constituting an inferior medium. It is not surprising, however, that some of its most ardent supporters were anarchists such as Aristide Bruant and the critic Félix Fénéon, who appreciated the idea of an art of the streets, constantly changing and non-exclusive in the audience it sought to address, where conventional aesthetic virtues were challenged, and which was cheap, essentially transient and constantly being updated.

The reality was somewhat different, and rather than subverting traditional notions of aesthetic acceptability, the lithograph was rapidly subsumed into the domain of high art. The vogue for posters in the 1890s was such that works were often stolen from their sites after dark, and their commercial potential was quickly realised. In 1893 Edouard Duchâtel published *Traité de lithographie artistique* and Lautrec often produced work for collectors' albums such as André Marty's *L'Estampe Originale* between 1893 and 1895. In 1895 Lautrec exhibited at the Centenaire de la Lithographie in Paris and frequently included his posters in exhibitions across Europe. Few of the formal devices he used in his lithographs were new – most were already apparent in his paintings before his first poster of 1891 – but the medium was ideally suited to a popularisation of his work and marked the start of Lautrec's reputation. Had he continued to work in oil and canvas it is unlikely that he would have been as favourably regarded by history as he has been, but his opportunistic use of lithograph guaranteed his contemporary and posthumous reputation in a way that was denied his avant-garde peers. Less than ten years after arriving in Paris Lautrec was fêted, famous at all levels of society and enjoying a steady income from his work.

Cover for *L'Estampe originale*,
1893
Lithograph, 56.5 x 64 cm

l'estampe
originale
publiée
par
le Journal des
artistes

Hautrec. 93

*Monsieur Delaporte at the Jardin
de Paris,* 1893
Cardboard, 76 x 70 cm
Copenhagen, NY Carlsberg
Glyptotek

Chapter 5

Publicity for the stars

In 1892 Aristide Bruant was engaged to appear at two other clubs, including the famous Eldorado, a variety hall where top entertainers played on the boulevard de Strasbourg, one of Haussmann's fashionable wide boulevards, and the Ambassadeurs, a café-concert on the rue Gabriel. In order to publicise these performances he commissioned Lautrec to produce posters advertising his appearance. The manager of the Ambassadeurs, Pierre Ducarre, refused to accept Lautrec's image, which he found 'a revolting mess' and commissioned one of his own from Georges Lévy. Bruant refused to perform if Lautrec's poster was not accepted. In the end it was a great success and Lautrec went on to design a number of other posters advertising Bruant's performances as well as the cover for a collection of his songs. Lautrec was fortunate in having the support of Bruant but the entertainer clearly appreciated the importance of simple, recognisable and memorable images to publicise his work and exploited that for his own ends. Lautrec's images are 'modern' in so far as they acknowledge the cynical transaction between the purveyor of the commodity and the advertising industry. Bruant was a consummate self-publicist, recognising and filling an important gap in the market with his risqué material and using the poster to appeal to a popular audience.

Aristide Bruant at Les Ambassadeurs (see p. 62) is a drawing for a projected poster that Lautrec eventually rejected in favour of a much starker image. It represents Bruant seen from behind, an unusual angle for the depiction of a performer – but one which had already been used on numerous occasions by Degas – because of the psychological vulnerability it suggested of the extrovert figure glimpsed at ease. Lautrec included two other figures, one of whom is identifiable as Jane Avril, but presumably the image was too cluttered and the final version is much simpler and more powerful. Another project for a poster of *Aristide Bruant* made in 1893 (see p. 65) is shown here in its first state, before the addition of any typography. The economy of means that represents this poster's greatest virtue is apparent only when it is compared with the drawings for the rejected schemes, and demonstrates Lautrec's laborious working methods hidden behind an understated nonchalance.

Other lithographs served quite different ends. *The Englishman at the Moulin Rouge* of 1892 developed out of a painting with the same title (Albi, Musée Toulouse-Lautrec) (see p. 63). It represents W.T. Warrener (1861–1934) who was in Paris studying at the Académie Julian. By 1889 this was one of a chain of free studios founded by Rodolphe Julian, which attracted over 600 students and where prominent members of the Nabi group and a number of foreigners, including George Moore, Lovis Corinth and William Rothenstein, came to study in the French capital. The study for

A Corner of the Moulin de la Galette, 1892
Cardboard on wood, 100.3 x 89.1 cm
Washington, National Gallery of
Art, Chester Dale Collection

the lithograph is painted in a mixture of gouache and oil on card and is a remarkably free representation of the scene (New York, Metropolitan Museum of Art). Lautrec has managed to retain some of that easy facility with line in the lithograph, passing off a remarkably contrived work with apparent ease. Mr Warrener himself is represented in one colour, like Désossé in *At the Moulin Rouge: La Goulue* (see p. 60), but the use of the *crachis* technique prevents any monotony. Lautrec had originally wanted the work to be entitled *The Flirt*, and this would imply that he intended it as a study in social mores. As the pose of the red-haired woman suggests that she is recoiling from Warrener's advances, such a title would at best have been equivocal.

Jane Avril

At the same time Lautrec continued to produce oil paintings and in 1892 painted several of Jane Avril (1868–1943), whom he had known since 1890 and with whom he remained friendly until the end of his life. One of the last posters he made was of her (see p. 70), and she seems to have been someone whom Lautrec could regard as an intimate. Socially, Lautrec was much closer to her than most of the other female performers – she was the daughter of a celebrated courtesan of the Second Empire and an Italian nobleman. She began her career as a dancer at the Moulin Rouge in 1889, where she was known by the nickname of La Mélinite, a new type of explosive, and from there she moved onto other Parisian clubs. After a period working in London and New York she finally gave up dancing in 1905 when she married.

In *Jane Avril Dancing* (see p. 68), a painting in oil on cardboard, she is shown dancing the quadrille. Mr Warrener is seated in the background. Unlike other dancers she preferred to work as a solo performer. The English poet Arthur Symons described her dancing as 'young and girlish, the more provocative because she played as a prude, with an assumed modesty ... and had about her a depraved virginity'.

The painting *Jane Avril leaving the Moulin Rouge* (see p. 66) shows the star after the performance is over, contemplative and forlorn. As a portrait, the work is little more than a caricature but as an image of the flipside of the gaiety of the dance-halls it is haunting, depicting the dancer self-contained and isolated, with her back turned to the bright lights of the Moulin Rouge. Painted on a cardboard ground, which is quite visible, and with a variety of strokes used throughout the work, ranging from the pointillist touch employed on the pavement to the long slashes of Avril's costume, the variety of texture and the influence of drawing is reminiscent of the work of Van Gogh.

Avril's infamous demureness and her characteristic enveloping clothing are used in the portrait *Jane Avril in the Entrance of the Moulin Rouge* (see p. 67), also painted in 1892. When compared with *La Goulue entering the Moulin Rouge* (see p. 72) of the same year, it can be seen that the difference between the two stars' character is vividly caught by Lautrec.

Papa Chrysanthème, 1892
Cardboard, 59 x 79 cm
Albi, Musée Toulouse-Lautrec

Papa Chrysanthème, 1892
Cardboard, 65 x 58.3 cm
Albi, Musée Toulouse-Lautrec

La Goulue and Valentin le Désossé

Lautrec's other favourite female star from the early 1890s was La Goulue (1870–1929), who emigrated to Paris from Alsace where she had been a laundress. After working at the Moulin de la Galette and the Jardin de Paris, she became the star attraction at Oller and Zidler's revamped Moulin Rouge. The lascivious display of her act was merely alluded to by Lautrec in his first poster *At the Moulin Rouge: La Goulue* (see p. 60), with her spinning legs forming the fulcrum for his composition. Her nickname, meaning 'The Glutton', and the psychological penetration of paintings such as *La Goulue entering the Moulin Rouge*, which shows the star arriving at the night-club, her arms linked with two other dancers, hint at the sensual pleasures which were responsible for her rapid decline. In this painting she was only in her early twenties but behind the bravura of her entrance Lautrec has captured something of the world-weariness of the young woman whose vaguely titillating acts had been responsible for catapulting her from poverty to luxury in a few short years.

In *Preparing for the Quadrille* of 1892 (see p. 75) Lautrec has once again situated the centre of attention in the middle of the painting, as he had done in works such as *The Dance at the Moulin Rouge* of 1890 (see p. 56), with abruptly attenuated foreground figures working as a *repoussoir* element in order to attract attention to the dancer at the opposite side of the painting. In building up his compositions in this way Lautrec is acknowledging the theatrical aspect of his work. Indeed, these works executed in the Moulin Rouge in the early 1890s use a limited pictorial vocabulary with great fluency, and it is in the posters, particularly *At the Moulin Rouge: La Goulue* that it works best. The acidic colours (suggested by the artificial lighting in the cabarets and theatres) contribute to the unreality of the whole, as does the caricatural treatment of the figures. Although La Goulue is recognisable here, she has been elevated to an archetype, functioning best when seen in opposition to her main rival, Jane Avril, whose performance depended upon a rather more cerebral appeal, which fact the proprietors of the Moulin Rouge were not slow to exploit for commercial ends.

By 1894 the quadrille had ceased to be popular, and La Goulue was already suffering from the effects of alcohol and was too overweight to continue dancing at the Moulin Rouge. The following year she gave a performance at the annual fair at Neuilly, where she had her own specially constructed pavilion decorated with works by Lautrec. On 6 April 1895 she wrote to him 'Dear friend ... my booth will be at the Foire du Trône – I have an excellent site and would be extremely pleased if you could find time to paint something for me ...'

Lautrec provided two panels for her booth: *La Goulue Dancing* (see p. 76) and *La Goulue dancing with Valentin le Désossé* (see p. 78). In the former La Goulue is shown in an imaginary scene, performing an exotic belly dance which had been imported into Paris at the Exposition Universelle of 1889 and which she adopted for her current show. In the audience, Lautrec has included Tinchant,

Loïe Fuller at the Folies-Bergère,
1893
Cardboard, 63.2 x 45.3 cm
Albi, Musée Toulouse-Lautrec

Paul Leclercq, 1897
Cardboard, 54 x 67 cm
Paris, Musée d'Orsay

the pianist from Le Chat Noir, the photographer Paul Sescau and the Irish writer Oscar Wilde, whom he had met probably in 1892, wearing a top hat, beside Jane Avril dressed in black. Next to her, Lautrec has depicted himself seen from behind, and at the right-hand side the writer Félix Fénéon, then working for the *Revue Blanche*.

The other canvas represents a scene from La Goulue's days at the Moulin Rouge with her dancing partner Valentin le Désossé. Both canvases were subsequently cut up but were restored by the Louvre, which acquired them in 1929.

By 1896 La Goulue's career had declined further and she began to compete in wrestling matches. In 1900 her performance included wild beasts as she desperately tried to regain some of her original power to shock, but she was unsuccessful and eventually worked as a servant in a brothel.

Yvette Guilbert

Apart from Jane Avril, the other female artiste with whom Lautrec remained on intimate terms until his death was Yvette Guilbert (1868–1944), who had first appeared in his work as the performer in his poster, the *Divan Japonais* of 1892, (see p. 73), depicting Jane Avril and the symbolist writer Edouard Dujardin. Guilbert is in the background and despite having no head in the poster (a device Manet used in his theatre scenes), the popular singer is immediately identifiable by the clinging gown and long black gloves which were her trademark. Lautrec probably met her at the end of that year as there is a letter from her written to him at the beginning of January 1893. The critic Gustave Geffroy, writing in *La Justice* on 15 February 1893, commented on the popularity of the artist's posters: 'Bruant, La Goulue and most recently Le Divan Japonais have taken possession of the street with an irresistible authority.'

The Divan Japonais pandered to the vogue for things oriental. It was a small café-concert on the rue des Martyrs with a pseudo-oriental decor of bamboo and Japanese lanterns, and waitresses and musicians dressed in kimonos. Guilbert had also worked at the Moulin de la Galette and the Jardin de Paris, but from 1889 she had worked exclusively at the more intimate café-concert. In an oil painting of 1894 Lautrec depicted *Yvette Guilbert taking a Curtain Call* (see p. 80) and in a study for a poster (see p. 81) he used the same rapid short-hand techniques to capture not only the omnipresent black gloves and low-cut dress but also the vivacious expression of the sharp wit which contributed to her success. The projected design never went any further than this rapid sketch, however, presumably because of Guilbert's dissatisfaction with her appearance in this work. She wrote to Lautrec: '... for the love of heaven, don't make me so dreadfully ugly! A little less so! A number of people uttered savage cries when they saw the coloured drawing here. Not everyone appreciates only the artistic qualities ...' In this last sentence Guilbert acknowledged the problem of finding a compromise between the flattery that official publicity grants the artiste, and the desire to construct a bold, recognisable image.

La Revue Blanche, 1895
Poster, 130 x 95 cm

In 1894 Lautrec collaborated with Gustave Geffroy on an album dedicated to Guilbert, in which he provided marginal illustrations to complement Geffroy's text. In all, there were sixteen lithographs and a cover which simply depicted *Yvette Guilbert's Black Gloves* (see p. 82), an image which not only acknowledges her most recognisable trait, but also suggests something of the transience of theatrical pleasures. The album was published by André Marty of *L'Estampe Originale* with a very small print run of only one hundred numbered copies. Reaction to it was mixed, with the split that Guilbert herself had recognised dividing the critics into those who praised its bold design and those who would have preferred something prettier. Others attacked it on the grounds that it accorded a popular entertainer an unmerited cult status.

Marcelle Lender

In February 1895 Hervé's operetta *Chilpéric* was revived at the Théâtre des Variétés, to wide success. Lautrec went to see it many times and produced a series of lithographs and an ambitious oil painting depicting its female star, Marcelle Lender (1862–1926). In the painting, *Marcelle Lender dancing the Bolero in 'Chilpéric'* (see p. 84), he has focused on one of the most exotic scenes from the musical, which is set in Merovingian times when the Frankish king Chilpéric watches while his Spanish bride Galswintha dances the bolero.

In 1895 Lautrec produced a lithograph, *Mlle Marcelle Lender* (see p. 83). This had been commissioned by the critic Julius Meier-Graefe for the German Neue Sezession magazine *Pan*, founded in 1895, and it appeared there in a large edition. The work was rather more complex than some of Lautrec's earlier lithographs, demonstrating his confidence in the medium. He used a larger number of colours than usual, superimposing them to create a wider variety of textures.

May Belfort

The Irish singer May Egan, who changed her name to May Belfort, had worked in London before coming to Paris in January 1895. She was employed, among other places, at the Cabaret des Décadents, a small café-concert on the rue Fontaine near the Moulin Rouge. She dressed in baby clothes and appeared on stage stroking a cat and singing songs redolent with innuendo:

> 'I've got a little cat
> And I'm very fond of that ...'

Her limited repertoire as *ingénue* meant that the appeal of her act was rather short-lived but, for a time, Lautrec was fascinated and made a set of six lithographs, including *May Belfort* (see p. 85). One of his most distinctive lithographs, it is in four colours – black, green, red and yellow – and includes a subtle use of *crachis*. After producing the poster in various editions for collectors, one of which includes the *remarque* in the upper right-hand corner of a cat wearing

Romain Coolus, 1899
Cardboard, 56.2 x 36.8 cm
Albi, Musée Toulouse-Lautrec

The Good Engraver: Adolphe Albert, 1898
Lithograph, 34.1 x 24.3 cm

a ruff, it was used to advertise the Petit-Casino. Lautrec included this work in the poster exhibition held at Reims in 1896.

In his representations of popular stars Lautrec helped to create and consolidate their reputations. Like a social satirist or caricaturist, he grasped salient features which he reiterated until they transcended the individual to whom they were originally attributed. In creating these popular icons he recognised the importance of understatement, absence of superficial prettiness, the cult of the personality and, particularly, mass circulation.

Napoléon, 1895
Poster, 59 x 45.2 cm

Chapter 6

Jardin de Paris

Although specialising in lithography, Lautrec continued to paint in oils, often returning to old themes in works such as *At 'La Mie'* (see p. 90), a café scene which is reminiscent of Degas' *L'Absinthe* of 1876 (see p. 25), although here Lautrec has included the added dimension of the male sitter's lecherous look directed at his female companion. This character was modelled by his friend Maurice Guibert (1856–1913), who worked as a champagne salesman and who made a number of trips with Lautrec, including visits to Malromé to see the Comtesse. According to an article in the journal *Fin de Siècle*, he was 'of the whole capital the man who knew the prostitutes best'. The woman has finished eating and appears to be on the point of leaving her chair, perhaps as the result of a suggestion by her calculating companion, who leans forward across the table. In this respect the theme is very close to that of *The Englishman at the Moulin Rouge*, where a similar transaction seems to have just been attempted. Despite this apparent informality the whole work is quite contrived, the painting being based on a photograph of the pair taken by Lautrec's friend Paul Sescau, who worked on the place Pigalle and for whom the artist designed a poster in 1894. Lautrec sent the work to the Salon des Indépendants, which along with Les XX (and after 1893 La Libre Esthétique) became the most important exhibiting venue for his work in the 1890s.

At the same time he made a number of trips abroad, including several to Spain in 1890, 1895 and again in 1896; to Belgium and Holland in 1894 and to London in 1892, 1894, 1895 and again in 1898. In London in 1894 with Joyant he met Oscar Wilde, who refused to sit for Lautrec, but he produced a portrait from memory and included him in the panel for La Goulue's booth at the Foire du Trône of 1895 (see p. 76).

He remained on intimate terms with his cousin Gabriel Tapié de Céleyran (1869–1930) (see p. 92), who had arrived in Paris in 1891 to study medicine at the Hôpital Saint Louis under Jules-Emile Péan (1830–1898). He also made a number of new friends, including *Romain Coolus* (1868–1952) (see p. 112), who worked at the *Revue Blanche* and with whom he visited a number of new clubs, including the Jardin de Paris on the Champs-Elysées, which was also founded by Oller and Zidler in 1893. Rather than rivalling their other establishments such as the Moulin Rouge, the Jardin de Paris was founded to complement it, and after the star turns such as Jane Avril and Yvette Guilbert finished work in the Montmartre club, they went down to the Jardin de Paris for a second session. It was there that Lautrec painted *Monsieur Delaporte at the Jardin de Paris* (see p. 100), a portrait of the manager of Delaporte and Chatard, an advertising and poster company on the rue Montmartre. In this intimate portrait, which he inscribed 'pour M. Delaporte – H.T. Lautrec', the artist has depicted the businessman against the backdrop of the club

La Passagère du 54, 1896
Lithograph, 59 x 39.7 cm

Marcelle, 1894
Cardboard, 46.5 x 29.5 cm
Albi, Musée Toulouse-Lautrec

Portrait of Louis Pascal, 1893
Cardboard, 81 x 54 cm
Albi, Musée Toulouse-Lautrec

and, like so many of his male figures, ostentatiously fingering his cane.

Gradually, Lautrec began to forsake his old haunts in Montmartre for the night life in the smarter area of Paris around the Champs-Elysées, although he kept his studio in the rue Caulaincourt until 1897. This happened partly as he changed his circle of friends but also in response to a change in subject-matter in his works. The multi-figured oil painting which had interested him in the late 1880s and early 1890s, such as *A Corner of the Moulin de la Galette* of 1892 (see p. 102) ceased to form the basis of his work and as he worked increasingly in lithography he became more interested in the single figure or a pair, and in a deeper psychological penetration of the individual.

Monsieur, Madame and a Dog,
1893
Canvas, 48 x 60 cm
Albi, Musée Toulouse-Lautrec

Lautrec made a series of lithographs of various scenes from the theatre, including *Sarah Bernhardt in 'Phèdre'* (see p. 94), a scene from Racine's drama. At this stage Bernhardt (1845–1923) was at the peak of her fame and commissioned posters advertising her work from a number of artists, including Eugène Grasset and Alphonse Mucha. It is odd, therefore, that she never commissioned one from Lautrec. He does not seem to have been interested in depicting her either, however, perhaps because her cult status made her seem distant and aloof – perhaps, also, because he was less interested in the theatre proper as opposed to the popular cabaret. This lithograph appeared in the short-lived illustrated periodical *L'Escarmouche* on 24 December 1893.

Loïe Fuller

Loïe Fuller (1862–1928) was an American dancer, born in Chicago, who made her début at the Folies-Bergère in October 1892. The Folies had been founded in 1869 as the Café du Sommier Elastique for vaudevilles and concerts, and Manet had set his last great Salon

painting *A Bar at the Folies-Bergère* of 1881 (see p. 153). As that painting shows, the establishment was frequented by a fairly affluent clientele, who went to see the theatrical spectacle as much as the more intimate café-concert. In 1889 the Folies went bankrupt and was bought by the Allemand family, who placed Edouard Marchand in charge. It was he who was responsible for transforming it into one of the most chic night-clubs in the capital, and he continually sought out new performers. Fuller's act (see p. 106) exploited the newly installed electric lights and the fashion for Art Nouveau, which sought to erode the distinction between the 'high' and 'low' arts and made use of the swirling arabesque for decorative effect, although the dealer Bing was not to open his shop in Paris with that name until the end of 1895. The performer entered the stage wearing voluminous drapery which she activated in intricate rhythms about her person by means of sticks held in her hands. For the Fire Dance or the Butterfly Dance, changing coloured lights were projected across the surface of the fabric, as Lautrec has attempted to suggest in this oil sketch.

In February 1893 Lautrec made a print of the same scene – his first lithograph which was not a poster. He took great pains with it, exercising more control than is normal in such a work, and fin-

The Laundryman, 1894
Cardboard, 57.8 x 46.2 cm
Albi, Musée Toulouse-Lautrec

ished it by hand, making each impression slightly differently coloured and with a dusting of gold or silver powder, presumably suggested to him by his study of Japanese prints.

Fuller's act created such a sensation that it generated a number of imitations, including the mock Japanese nautical ballet *Papa Chrysanthème* (see p. 104) at the Nouveau Cirque (another Oller establishment), in which the dancers wore similar costumes, performing on a giant lotus leaf in the centre of a pool of water. It was perhaps because of such emulation that Fuller patented her act in 1894.

The *Revue Blanche*

From 1893 Lautrec produced work for the *Revue Blanche*, one of the most important innovatory magazines in Paris in the 1890s, based on the rue Laffitte, and the mouthpiece of the Symbolist writers. It had been founded in 1889 by the writer Paul Leclercq, who was its first editor and who subsequently wrote a biography of the artist, *Autour de Toulouse-Lautrec* (1921). This book details the procedure Lautrec adopted in his portrait of *Paul Leclercq* in 1897 (see p. 109). He visited the artist's studio in the avenue Frochot about twenty times: 'I have a very clear recollection that I posed no more than two or three hours ... He peered at me through his eye-glasses, screwed up his eyes, took his brush, and having made a thorough examination of what he wanted to see, used diluted paint to make two or three light brush-strokes upon the canvas ...'

The title *Revue Blanche* referred to the absence of any editorial control over the contents and it attracted a wide spectrum of writers, including established figures such as Zola, as well as Ibsen, Mallarmé and Proust. Although it was primarily a literary magazine, each edition of the *Revue Blanche* included an original lithograph as a frontispiece. In 1891 it was taken over by the Polish Natanson brothers, Alexandre (1867–1936) and Thadée (1868–1951), who co-edited it with some help from the third brother, Louis-Alfred. By the beginning of 1894 and for the next three years, Lautrec was an intimate of the circle around them which included Romain Coolus and the anarchist Félix Fénéon, who was implicated in the so-called 'Trial of the Thirty', a trial of thirty leading anarchists in August 1895 after the bombing of the Café Terminus by Emile Henry. Although there was sufficient evidence to indict Fénéon, he was acquitted after having engaged in a verbal jousting match with the prosecution. Fénéon's political beliefs were widely recognised but do not seem to have stood in the way of friendship with Lautrec, who portrayed the recognisable figure in his decoration for La Goulue's fair booth, along with Oscar Wilde, who also underwent trial in May 1895 but with a less successful outcome. Both men were charismatic figures with a sharp and often caustic wit, and their beliefs do not seem to have detracted from the artist's admiration for them.

In an advertising poster for the *Revue Blanche* that he produced in 1895 Lautrec used Thadée Natanson's wife Misia, née Godebska, (1872–1950) as his model (see p. 110). Printed in four colours –

In Bed, 1892
Cardboard on panel, 54 x 70.5 cm
Paris, Musée d'Orsay

blue, red, green and black – it marks a departure from earlier, bolder images such as *Aristide Bruant* (see p. 65). There is a greater awareness of texture and more emphasis is placed on line, often for decorative ends as in the plumes in her hat and the fur of her muff and collar of her skating costume. In style as well as in sentiment it is much closer to Art Nouveau. This tendency towards the kind of rhythmic prettiness associated with Art Nouveau is also apparent in the lithograph published by the *Journal des Artistes* in 1893 for *L'Estampe Originale* (see p. 99), a magazine first published on 30 March 1893. It represents Jane Avril examining a lithographic proof, with the printer working the press in the background, and demonstrates the importance placed on lithography by this date. Lautrec also painted Misia Natanson's half-brother Cipa Godebski (1865–1909) (see p. 94), who was the son of the Polish sculptor Cyprian Godebski and a member of the *La Revue Blanche* circle. The artist met him at Villeneuve-sur-Yonne where he was a guest of the Natansons in 1896.

Other lithographs from around this time demonstrate the same stylisation with a tendency towards more elegant line than in earlier works. *La Passagère du 54* (see p. 116) makes use of the same kind of refinement found in *La Revue Blanche* (see p. 110) and an increasingly complex use of colour – here, six different colours were used, necessitating individual stones. The subject was a passenger occupying cabin number 54 whom Lautrec had observed while on board the steamer *Le Chili* from Bordeaux to Lisbon with Maurice Guibert. In its third state the lithograph was used as a poster to advertise the Salon des Cents.

Napoleon

In the spring of 1895 Lautrec entered a competition organised by the art dealers Boussod and Valadon, intended to find a designer for a poster advertising a biography of Napoleon I by W. Milligan Sloane to be published in the *Century Magazine* in New York the following year. The winner was to receive a cash prize and a trip to New York. The competition was judged by Detaille, Gérome and Vibert, who chose a design by Lucien Métiviet. Lautrec came third and had one hundred copies of his poster (see p. 114) printed at his own expense. It was produced in five colours – blue, reddish brown, yellow and a pale grey applied with a brush and a darker grey with the lithographic crayon. The design betrays the original destination of the work and it is demonstrably less adventurous than his other works, being much more illustrative, with attention paid to the drawing, particularly of the horses. Perhaps it was annoyance at not having taken first prize that caused him to undertake this project, which he had to finance himself. Certainly, given Lautrec's political beliefs, the subject-matter does not seem to have been one that interested him greatly.

Chapter 7

The Maisons closes

Although Lautrec continued to maintain a studio in Montmartre, after 1891 he began to spend more time in the fashionable brothels of the capital, sometimes lodging there for several weeks at a stretch. These were on the rue des Moulins off the avenue de l'Opéra, on the rue d'Amboise off the boulevard des Italiens, and on the rue Joubert behind the Opéra. In other words, all were situated in the area of the Grands Boulevards built by Haussmann and one of the most fashionable districts of the capital, quite different from the working-class milieu of Montmartre. Increasingly his subject-matter was drawn from the opulent brothel or *maison close*, and there is something to suggest that it provided him with the same kind of material that had interested him in the work he produced in the cabarets and cafés-concerts earlier in his career. As he moved away from the multi-figured compositions of his earliest works, such as *The Dance at the Moulin Rouge* of 1890 (see p. 56), Lautrec began to seek out the more telling psychological revelations of individual performers, often shown as unexpectedly lonely and introspective, such as *Jane Avril leaving the Moulin Rouge* (see p. 66).

That both types of subject-matter provided the basis for a rich social allegory would not have been lost on him, and indeed writers of the Second Empire had constantly used the figure of the prostitute as a metaphor for a society in decline. Edmond de Goncourt's *La Fille Elisa* of 1877 or Emile Zola's *Nana* of 1880 can both be read as mildly titillating accounts of a courtesan whose downward progress is charted as she sinks further in society and her immoral ways reap their just deserts. Certainly, that was the kind of moral a bourgeois audience sought, with the fallen woman presented as the antithesis of the virtuous mother and wife. But the implications of the novel were wider, and could be construed as a comment on the rotten state of French society.

Artists too had dealt with the theme – Thomas Couture's *Romans of the Decadence* (Paris, Musée d'Orsay), as well as being a huge Salon success, was widely recognised, in its depiction of a courtesan holding court at an orgy, to be a metaphor for the decline into which the Second Empire had sunk. Both Courbet and Manet had chosen the theme of the prostitute for some of the most enduring and influential images in French art, with which Toulouse-Lautrec would have been well acquainted. Interestingly, Manet's *Olympia* (see p. 137) does not provide its prurient bourgeois audience with any easy sermonising: the courtesan that it represents is shown as being commercially successful, with little apparent guilt. And, of course, Degas had produced some of the best-known and most intimate images of prostitutes in their everyday milieu in a series of works.

Paris was much more liberal in its approach to prostitution than some of its European neighbours at the end of the nineteenth century, partly out of a kind of hypocritical necessity. In 1892 it had

Femme de Maison, 1894
Panel, 22.5 x 16 cm
Albi, Musée Toulouse-Lautrec

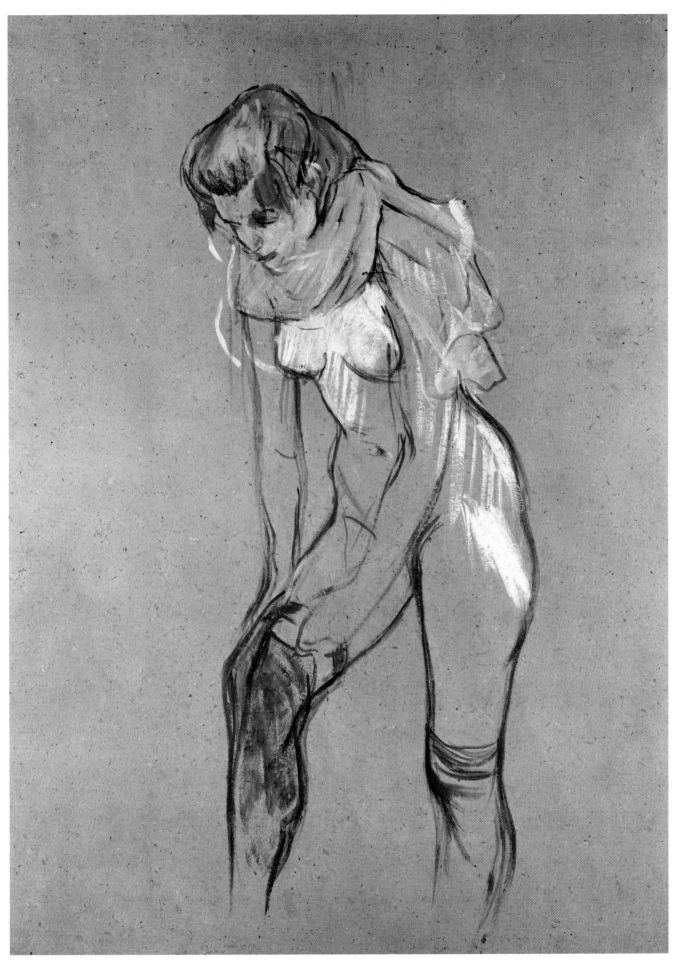

Woman Pulling up her Stocking, 1894
Cardboard, 61.5 x 44.5 cm. Albi, Musée Toulouse-Lautrec

Woman Pulling up her Stocking,
Detail

129

Lautrec and nude model admiring
The Salon at the rue des Moulins

*The Salon at the rue des
Moulins,*1894
Canvas, 111.5 x 132.5 cm
Albi, Musée Toulouse-Lautrec

The Friends, 1894
Cardboard, 48 x 34.5 cm
Albi, Musée Toulouse-Lautrec

A Passing Fancy, 1896
Canvas, 103 x 65 cm
Toulouse, Musée des Augustins

fifty-nine brothels which were strictly regulated by the French state, but there was a large number of unregistered establishments that were largely uncontrolled. In all, Paris supported 34,000 prostitutes compared with London's 24,000, with only half of its population. Statistics are difficult to validate, but any figures can be based only on official numbers who registered in the annual *Guide Rose*: there was a whole underbelly of amateur or part-time women whose activities were never monitored. For working women, particularly immigrants from the provinces who were employed as waitresses or laundresses, occasional prostitution was often their only means of alleviating hardship and poverty. Fictional works by Maupassant or Zola deal with the *grisette*, the young working-class woman who tried to better herself socially by taking a permanent lover from the ranks of the bourgeoisie, rather than a string of clients. Certain occupations, presumably because of their low pay and the large number of immigrants that they employed, seemed to have been associated with prostitution. Lautrec's *The Laundress* is typ-

133

ical of the type of young woman for whom occasional prostitution was a necessity. The need to turn to prostitution was based on both economic and social considerations and this further emphasised the perceived split between the virtuous bourgeois wife and mother and the vicious prostitute with whom her husband sought pleasure.

Lautrec's family was no different from most other members of their class. After his parents effectively separated in 1868 there is nothing to suggest that the Comte would have ceased the womanising ways that had plagued their marriage, and he took great delight in introducing his only son to the pleasures of Paris. At the same time, Lautrec's images of his mother portray her as a refined woman, eyes demurely diverted from the viewer, always indoors and performing the most mundane of domestic rituals. Lautrec's letters to the Comtesse betray this same protective and prescriptive approach to femininity, and there is a great deal in them to suggest that he idolised her. Contemporary commentators have suggested that she was an exceedingly pious woman.

In 1892 Lautrec was commissioned by the *patronne* of a *maison close* in the rue d'Amboise to decorate one of the large salons used as a dining-room. The style chosen was intended to complement the Louis XV furnishings of the place and was presumably at his patron's request. In all, he provided sixteen oval medallions set in rococo cornices, each depicting one of the girls who worked there, garlanded with flowers. As an exercise in decoration the works are less than successful, and they have subsequently been dispersed. However, other paintings, drawings and prints which aim to provide a glimpse into the everyday life of the brothel are more fortunate, and some of them are touching representations of those on the edges of society.

The Laundryman of 1894 (see p. 122) is almost caricatural in its juxtaposition of the large figure of the decorously clad woman to the left-hand side and the lascivious leer of the man as he picks up the bag of laundry. It is one of the few depictions of brothel life where there is a man represented, and here the relationship between the figures is ambivalent. In other works the male presence is implied, perhaps by the inclusion of a top hat or a cane against a chair, or implicitly understood to be located outside the picture space. In establishing a narrative between what is represented in the works and the spectator, Lautrec is taking the lead in particular from paintings such as Manet's *Olympia* (see p. 137). The latter's work had been shown at a huge retrospective in 1884, a year after his death.

Other works studiously avoid any voyeuristic implications. One depicts the women queuing up for their routine medical examinations in an unobtrusive, yet not coldly clinical way. This is a reminder that these establishments were often strictly controlled because of the very real fear of syphilis, with its threat of madness and death. It has been estimated that as many as fifteen per cent of the deaths in France at the turn of the century were from syphilis and Lautrec himself had contracted it, probably in 1888. While he lived with Dr Bourges he received treatment for it, but after the physician's marriage he allowed it to lapse. Gonorrhoea was even more widespread.

La Toilette, 1896
Cardboard, 67 x 54 cm
Paris, Musée d'Orsay

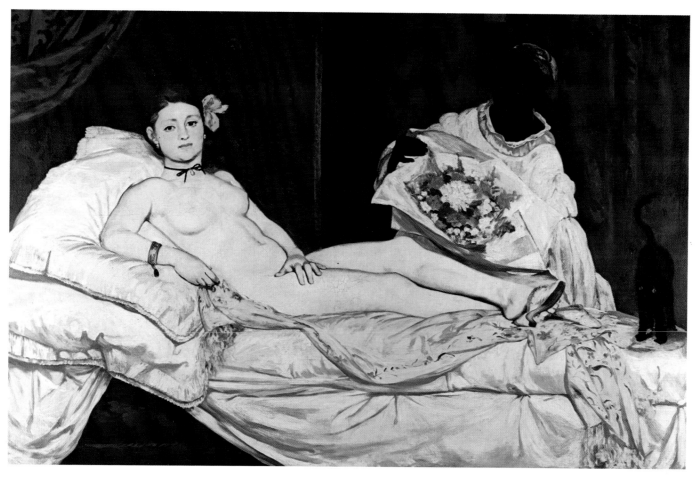

Edouard Manet, 1832-1883
Olympia, 1863
Canvas, 90 x 130.5 cm
Paris, Musée d'Orsay

Monsieur, Madame and a Dog of 1893 (see p. 120) depicts, according to Joyant, the proprietors of a brothel. The plush interior – a large mirror behind them suggests something of what is happening in the room – is at odds with their petit-bourgeois appearance. In this work, as in so many of the others, Lautrec has stressed the pedestrian nature of the brothel in unflattering yet sympathetic terms, with none of the moralising which would have made it more acceptable to a wider audience.

Paintings such as *Woman Pulling up her Stocking* (see p. 128), usually identified as a picture of a prostitute, have nothing to distinguish them from a conventional depiction of the artist's model. Indeed, the very neutrality of the subject seems to make it less touching and more academic in its practice.

Generally regarded as the climax of the pictures depicting the *maison close* in the rue des Moulins, *The Salon at the rue des Moulins* of 1894 (see p. 130) is a complex work in terms of its preparation and composition. There are a number of preparatory drawings and two versions of the finished work. Returning to the format of works such as *Dance at the Moulin de la Galette* of 1889 (see p. 48), the figures are kept at a distance from the spectator by a bank of velvet sofas, and the figures are artfully arranged to be viewed full-face or in profile. The figure with her chemise hitched round her waist is cut off at the extreme right-hand side of the work, foiling any opportunity for voyeurism. The informal attitude of the woman and the furnishings of the Salon serve as a reminder that the brothel was more than simply a milieu for sexual transactions. It was also a place of entertainment and relaxation, somewhere that flattered the ego of its tired customer and provided the pleasures of home

Mlle Lucie Bellanger, 1896
Cardboard, 80.7 x 60 cm
Albi, Musée Toulouse-Lautrec

Nude in front of a Mirror, 1897
Cardboard, 62.8 x 48 cm
New York, private collection

life with none of the attendant responsibilities. A contemporary photograph (see p. 131) shows Lautrec examining the painting in his studio with a model on the opposite side of the canvas. It is an important record: not only does it show other identifiable works such as *Monsieur, Madame and a Dog* (see p. 120) and *Alfred la Guigne* (see p. 140) but it also gives us some idea of how the work was originally displayed in a simple wooden frame that had first been favoured by artists in the Impressionist circle in the 1870s and 1880s. It is odd that Lautrec should have chosen not to exhibit such a major work during his lifetime. Perhaps it was so unequivocal in its depiction of a brothel that he was restrained by some misplaced social nicety.

In January 1896 Lautrec had an important one-man exhibition at the Manzi-Joyant gallery on the rue Forest, off the boulevard de Clichy. A number of brothel pictures were included but were displayed in two locked rooms and only his closest friends were allowed to see them. This is a further illustration of how the private persona differs radically from the wild hedonist of popular mythology.

In many of these representations Lautrec's presence (and the

140

implied presence of any male viewer or customer) is so understated and unobtrusive that one is forced to enquire about his relationship with these women. In a series of caricatures and sketches of himself in erotic situations, Lautrec was at great pains to emphasise his virility. Perhaps in compensation for his physical deformity, Lautrec referred to himself in grandiose terms in these sexual works, often pairing himself with women who were largely unattainable, such as Grenier's wife, Lily. Perhaps their tone should be regarded as ironical, but in painting and drawing women, he exercised a control over them which was more than merely sexual; his role as creator means that he could manipulate them for his own ends. It is in this role that he has been represented in the photograph, standing with his model in front of *The Salon at the rue des Moulins* (see p. 130). The equivocal relationship between the fully dressed artist at the right-hand side who gazes at the nude model to the left-hand side, who in turn contemplates the object of creation, turns what at first looks like an important historical document into a construction no less premeditated than the paintings it depicts. At the same time, Lautrec recognised the alienating nature of commercialised sex, a theme to which he had not been unsympathetic in earlier works such as *The Laundress* of 1889 (see p. 30).

Elles

In April 1896 Gustave Pellet published a series of ten lithographs entitled *Elles* with a cover and frontispiece by Toulouse-Lautrec. Originally called *La Fille* (The Tart), it was printed on handmade Japanese paper and the portfolio cost three hundred francs, or thirty-five francs per print, in a numbered edition of one hundred. The series is the product of the time between 1891 and 1895 that Lautrec had spent in brothels, and often draws on the repertoire of images that he had studied there. Like the paintings, these coloured lithographs were intended to depict the everyday life of prostitutes, showing them in bed or performing their toilet, often drawing on imagery that had been previously explored by Degas. Only the frontispiece did not depict a woman in a brothel; this was of the clowness Cha-U-Kao, whom Lautrec portrayed on a number of other occasions (see p. 146).

Once again there was little in the works that would have identified these women specifically as prostitutes, and the women are rarely seen engaging in any kind of transaction with clients. Lautrec was above all concerned with representing the daily life behind the opulent façade of the brothel. *A Passing Fancy* (see p. 133) is a painted version of one of these prints in which a woman, seen from behind, is seated at her dressing table putting on her corset, watched by her top-hatted client in the corner. The work is reminiscent of Manet's painting of *Nana* (see p. 47) and demands the same kind of literary interpretation. The coquetry of Manet's work has disappeared, however, and although the commercial relationship between the dandified figure of the man and the working woman is unambiguous, it has been handled in a way that is almost sympathetic to the woman. It is she who dominates the picture space; the kind of anonymity

Alfred la Guigne, 1894
Cardboard, 65.6 x 50.4 cm
Washington, National Gallery of Art,
Chester Dale Collection

Maxime Dethomas at the Opéra Ball, 1896
Cardboard, 67.3 x 52.7 cm
Washington, National Gallery of Art, Chester Dale Collection

that is suggested by her pose heightens the sense of the dehumanising nature of her work and the title suggests the outcome of their brief liaison. Not for the first time Lautrec has used a friend, here the artist Charles Conder, to epitomise a less than attractive aspect of male behaviour.

Despite being the highpoint of Lautrec's lithographic style and an attempt at a kind of reportage that exceeded the work of some of the Naturalist writers, the *Elles* series was neither a commercial nor a critical success, perhaps because it did not supply bourgeois morality with platitudes nor did it aim to be charming. These two objections, which could be levelled against all Lautrec's depictions of prostitutes, were summed up by his friend Gustave Geffroy, with whom he had collaborated on the Yvette Guilbert album, and who wrote in 1896:

'... a first objection could be made against the willingness to seek out and to increase ugliness. It is doubtless justified, but it is hardly necessary to generalise. There is an innate sense of caricature in Lautrec's work and to restrain it would be a great pity, because it is rich in pertinent revelations about social pretensions and moral defects ...

'As for a second objection sometimes raised, I shall strive even more to combat that. It tends to present as cynical, if not obscene, a number of characters and aspects of the so-called life of pleasure, that of prostitution. It is impossible for me to take such an impression away from these scenes. The concern for truth is overriding here, and is much stronger than all the inquisitiveness and all the intentions of those who look at them. Without any weird spectacles and without any nightmares, with only the wish to treat falsehood and the desire to expose the truth, Lautrec has created terrifying works, has cast the cruellest of lights on one of the hells of misery and vice hidden by our outward show of civilisation. Never has the pathetic profligacy, the passive stupidity, the animal unconsciousness, and also, what is the greatest sadness of all, the possibility for so many of these women with naïve countenance of a happy, regular, simple life, all of that has never been expressed with such a vividness, a tranquillity that is also searing.'

In the *Elles* series Lautrec extended the same kind of detachment to his female models as he did when portraying controversial male figures such as Fénéon or Wilde. Contrary to the kind of narrow-minded view of his class and his provincial upbringing, he did not presume to judge people in his art. Nowhere was this more evident than in his paintings of lesbians.

The lesbian pictures

Lautrec seems to have begun his studies of the lesbian relationships that existed between the women in the *maisons closes* as early as 1892. Unlike a frankly titillating work such as the euphemistically entitled *The Sleepers* of 1866 by Gustave Courbet (Paris, Musée du Petit Palais) which is directed at an exclusively male audience and is about the relationship between the women depicted and the spectator, Lautrec's representations of lesbians explore the rela-

143

La Grande Loge, 1896-1897
Cardboard, 55 x 47 cm
Private collection

tionship between the women themselves. One of the earliest is *In Bed* of 1892 (see p. 124), one of four pictures of the same two women. Far from the exploitative relationships that were hinted at in *A Passing Fancy* (see p. 133), the focusing on the tousled heads in the sea of the bed suggests a kind of security that was lacking from the prostitutes' commercial relationships with their clients. The immediacy of the scene and the unglamorised heads suggest a kind of reportage, but it is questionable to what extent Lautrec would have been allowed access to this kind of intimate scene. *The Friends* (see p. 132), however, is set in the public glare of the Salon and explores the companionship that existed between the women rather than any kind of salacious exchange. They are swaddled in drapery and the effect is quite different from the nudity of Courbet's *The Sleepers*.

Representations of women

Later works, although often not dealing specifically with prostitutes, draw their inspiration from the groundwork that Lautrec put in while staying in the brothels between 1891 and 1895. *Elsa la Viennoise* (see p. 134), a coloured lithograph from 1897, depicts a magnificently dressed prostitute descending the staircase of the brothel in the rue des Moulins. The range of textures is extraordinary here, from the loosely brushed design on her skirt to the rapid, nervous hatching that covers most of the surface of the stone, and then a haziness achieved by the use of *crachis* over large areas.

Others return to old themes; for example, in *Mlle Lucie Bellanger* of 1896 (see p. 138) Lautrec used a prostitute as his model for a view of a woman seen from behind. It is a confidently painted work which uses the minimum of strokes to achieve a powerful presence. Like *Woman Pulling up her Stocking* (see p. 126) which is very similarly executed, it seems incidental that it was posed by a prostitute, for she adopts the conventional attitude of a studio model, with her chemise slipped off her shoulder.

This interest in backs, both as the basis of anatomical studies and for the feeling of anonymity they help to create in his models, was used to great effect in one of Lautrec's most finished works of the female nude, *La Toilette* of 1896 (see p. 136). It is one of a number of similar works that he painted that year but differs in that it is much more realised in its execution. He has still favoured the cardboard support that formed the basis for his studies, and the diluted paint, which in places is dribbled on like water-colour, but in terms of representing a background that gives some insight into the intimacy of daily life, this work is quite unlike studies such as *Mlle Lucie Bellanger*. This effect is heightened by the untidy aspect of the room. Coupled with the impersonalised, ungainly pose as the artist towers over his model and the claustrophobic setting that this entails, the work is very reminiscent of the work of Degas. In fact, the use of dilute oil paint or *essence* was favoured by the older artist and it was not the first time that Lautrec had imitated him both in terms of subject-matter, treatment and medium. The use of colour is very sophisticated, with the cool blues of the linen offset against the warm reds and oranges, flecked with green and violet, of the model's hair.

The importance of Manet

Another highly finished work is the so-called *At the Rat Mort* (see p. 148), which derives its title from the restaurant of that name at

146

The Female Clown Cha-U-Kao,
1895
Cardboard, 64 x 49 cm
Paris, Musée d'Orsay

7 rue Pigalle which Lautrec frequented towards the end of his life with friends such as Charles Conder. It was a fashionable haunt of lesbians and the woman depicted here was a famous courtesan, Lucy Jourdain. It was unusual for Lautrec to paint a high-class prostitute. Just as he seems to have been uninterested in painting *Sarah Bernhardt in 'Phèdre'*(see p. 98) as an embodiment of the respected high theatre, preferring instead the artistes of the more popular cafés-concerts, so too does he seem to have favoured the demi-mondaine's lower-class counterparts. It is a rich and sumptuous painting, working on the complementaries green and red, and the handling is noticeably more fluid than in earlier works. Rapid hatching on Jourdain's clothing contrasts with the baroque flourishes of the fruit and bowl in the foreground. The uplighting on the model's face is a refinement of the rather crude colouring of the foreground figure in *At the Moulin Rouge* of 1892 (see p. 58). A comparison between these two works demonstrates a return to a much more painterly execution in the later picture, which may seem surprising, given the experimentation in posters and prints that had occupied him in the intervening years, but as *Elsa la Viennoise* (see p. 134) demonstrates, he had begun to move away from the bold flat design of the earlier lithographs, such as *Aristide Bruant* (see p. 65). The man in the painting is usually identified as Charles Conder, and the summary attenuation of his face and body suggest the dandy in Manet's *Nana* (see p. 47). Alongside the constant presence of Degas, the influence of Manet is evident in this and other representations of prostitutes, not only in formal devices such as this but, more important, for the kind of transaction that that implies. A work such as *Maxime Dethomas at the Opéra Ball* of 1896 (see p. 142) which is ostensibly a portrait formally similar to *Monsieur Delaporte at the Jardin de Paris* of three years earlier (see p. 100) in fact transcends simple portrait and becomes much closer in theme to *The Englishman at the Moulin Rouge*. Like the representation of Monsieur Dethomas, the man seated in the foreground forms a counterpoise to the pink figures in the scene behind. Monsieur Dethomas (1868–1928), a painter and stage designer, appears unperplexed; only the empty glass at the edge of the table and his tightly grasped cane suggest his interest.

Alfred la Guigne (see p. 140) depicts a fictional character from the novel by Oscar Méténier to whom Lautrec inscribed the work 'pour Méténier d'après son Alfred la Guigne'. Méténier had written a book on Bruant in 1893. Showing la Guigne standing at a bar with two women, one of whom is in riding costume, the work circumscribes the same world that Manet had depicted in *At the Café* of 1878 (Winterthur, Oskar Reinhart Collection). By the end of the nineteenth century Manet, the darling of the avant-garde in the 1860s, had been accorded his rightful place in French art. A major retrospective had been held after his death in 1884, and the dealer Durand-Ruel had mounted an exhibition of his work in 1896.

In its use of the cut-off of the nude to the right-hand side and the disjunction between the woman standing in the room and her reflection in the glass, *Nude in front of a Mirror* of 1897 (see p. 139) is reminiscent of Manet's work, especially the *Bar at the Folies-Bergère* (see p. 153). This dichotomy between the upright figure

At the Rat Mort, 1899
Canvas, 55.1 x 46 cm
London, Courtauld Institute
Galleries

Madame Berthe Bady, 1897
Cardboard, 70.3 x 60 cm
Albi, Musée Toulouse-Lautrec

Cha-U-Kao at the Moulin Rouge, 1895
Canvas, 75 x 55 cm
Winterthur, Oskar Reinhart
Collection

The Violinist Dancla, 1900
Canvas, 92 x 67 cm
Private collection

and her slouched reflection manages to evoke a sense of the split between the public persona and the private individual. Because of the shadowy nature of the reflection, it also manages to convey the eventual outcome of the woman. This theme of worldly transience had been used in earlier works, most noticeably in the early *Self-Portrait* (see p. 8). The sense of Lautrec's identification with prostitutes and people on the margins of society is all the more poignant since by this time he was suffering seriously from alcoholism and syphilis.

Cha-U-Kao

In all, Lautrec produced four oil paintings of the clowness Cha-U-Kao, whose name was a pseudo-oriental adaptation of her stage name, Chahut-Chaos. She worked at the Moulin Rouge and at the Nouveau Cirque in the rue Saint-Honoré. Founded in 1866, this

152

Edouard Manet, 1832-1883
Bar at the Folies-Bergère, 1882
Canvas, 96 x 130 cm
London, Courtauld Institute
Galleries

was hugely popular because of its pioneering use of machinery which enabled the circus ring to be transformed into a pool for aquatic presentations, including a mock Venetian carnival with gondolas. Other attractions included bullfights as well as the usual circus features. *Cha-U-Kao at the Moulin Rouge* of 1895 (see p. 150) depicts the female clown with the figure of Gabrielle la Danseuse, who seems to have modelled for some of Lautrec's representations of prostitutes. The work was displayed at Lautrec's one-man show at Joyant's gallery in 1896, the same year that he produced a lithograph of her to form the frontispiece to the *Elles* series. *The Female Clown Cha-U-Kao,* also painted in 1895 (see p. 146), represents her from behind in an oddly contorted pose, as she adjusts the yellow ruff that formed part of her costume. On the wall in the background a half-eaten snack lies on a little table and above it the soberly clad figure of a male protector is reflected in a mirror, suggesting the presence of a companion in the dressing–room after the evening's performance. Formally and thematically it is the female equivalent of *Maxime Dethomas at the Opéra Ball* (see p. 142). In both works, Lautrec has suggested the trade that existed between female artistes who attracted admirers and lovers from the ranks of the middle classes who attended their shows.

At the Bar, 1898
Cardboard, 81.5 x 60 cm
Zurich, Kunsthaus

Woman at her Toilet:
Mme Poupoule, 1898
Panel, 60.8 x 49.6 cm
Albi, Musée Toulouse-Lautrec

Chapter 8

The crisis of 1899

Lautrec's health began to deteriorate rapidly from about 1896. His illness meant that he was never strong, the syphilis from which he had suffered since about 1888 went untreated after he stopped living with Dr Bourges in 1893 and his addiction to alcohol became more marked. In 1897, while staying with his friends the Natansons at Villeneuve-sur-Yonne, he seems to have suffered from hallucinations and frightened his hosts by firing his gun at imaginary animals.

It has already been described how syphilis was endemic in France at the end of the nineteenth century. It was frequently perceived by the general public to be linked with alcoholism and this was perpetuated in fictional works. Zola's *L'Assommoir* of 1877 dealt with the problem of alcoholism but there it was presented as a working-class illness, one of the products of industrialisation and hence incurable. However, it affected the upper classes equally, at a time when the average annual consumption of wine was 208 litres. Lautrec did not confine himself to drinking wine, although his letters home often request crates to be sent to him, but in the night-clubs that he frequented he favoured a cocktail which he nicknamed 'un tremblement de terre' (an earthquake), a potent mixture of cognac and absinthe.

The breakdown from which Lautrec suffered at the beginning of 1899 was caused by a mixture of these symptoms, but seems to have been precipitated by his mother's sudden departure from Paris to Albi. They had always been close and their letters reveal that even when they both lived in Paris he would write to her and visit frequently, taking his meals with her. Clearly her son's behaviour, always a little erratic, had become embarrassing and she suddenly left Paris unannounced on 3 January, leaving her servant Berthe Sarrazin to look after her apartment on the rue de Douai and to report to her about Lautrec's behaviour. She also left her son 1,000 francs, which can only be construed as a bribe. The letters from Sarrazin to the Comtesse chronicle a deterioration in Lautrec's mental and physical health and recount symptoms that included delirium tremens and hallucinations. His mother seems to have been largely impervious to such reports as she remained in Albi despite appealing letters from her servant.

Sarrazin's first letter to the Comtesse is dated 4 January, the day after her mistress left Paris. She reported how on the previous evening she went to visit 'Monsieur Henri' who, on discovering that his mother had left, 'was very angry; he thumped the ground with his cane and swore ... I went to see him at 8 o'clock this morning and he was much calmer although he continued to say things that don't make sense. He has burned several newspapers in the toilet bowl again, but he is much better, nevertheless.'

The following day, Sarrazin wrote to another servant at Albi,

The Englishwoman at the 'Star',
Le Havre, 1899
Panel, 41 x 32.8 cm
Albi, Musée Toulouse-Lautrec

Adeline Cromont, and confided in her some of the things that she kept hidden from the Comtesse, such as how the artist had 'bought lots of things, old cake moulds, spoons for twenty francs at the colour merchants ...' and how he had spent the 1,000 francs his mother had left for him in one drunken evening. This kind of defiant gesture suggests Lautrec's unhappiness at being apparently abandoned by his mother. Letters from Sarrazin over the next few days chronicle his compulsive spending, a self-inflicted wound to his hand on the stove and how he has started applying glycerine and vaseline to his pictures with an old sock. His drinking continued and his constant companions on binges were Edmond Calmèse, the proprietor of a nearby livery stable, and a prostitute, 'Big Gabrielle', both of whom Sarrazin suspected of fleecing Lautrec.

Neither Dr Bourges nor Dr Gabriel Tapié de Céleyran, whom Sarrazin consulted about Lautrec, was able to suggest a course of action. Indeed, she reported to his mother on 30 January 1899 that he had started to suspect his cousin: '... he said to me that if he came, to drive him out of the door with the broom, or to lock him in a room, and to go and find him, and that he would see to him'. In a letter the following day to her confidante Cromont in Albi, Sarrazin confided that 'at the moment Monsieur has persecution mania'. Her use of such technical terms gives the reader some indication of the relatively sophisticated approach to various types of madness in France at the end of the century.

The kind of taxonomic interest in mental illness in France at that time meant that people who suffered from a wide variety of different symptoms were often perceived as being mad, although previously the same behaviour would simply have been classified as erratic. During the Second Empire and the Third Republic the number of certifiably insane rose quite dramatically. At its high point, one was eight times more likely to suffer from mental illness as from consumption, although statistics from mental asylums make no real distinction between long-term and senile patients and those who were interned only for a month or so. Alcohol-related madness, which accounted for a large number of such patients, was widely considered to be incurable. By the end of the century it was recognised that intermarrying gave rise to an increased tendency to madness, and such knowledge must have exacerbated his parents' guilt and embarrassment at their son's behaviour.

The prisoner

Acting against the advice of friends and family, the Comtesse had her son committed to an asylum in March in order to undergo a programme of detoxification. This was the luxurious sanatorium for nervous diseases La folie Saint James, set in the middle of gardens at 16 avenue de Madrid in Neuilly-sur-Seine and run by Dr Sémelaigne. Although Lautrec responded well to the detoxification and became lucid again, the kind of mistrust that this involuntary incarceration provoked must have soured already strained relations with his mother. In his memoirs, his friend Joyant makes it clear that the same results could have been achieved by rest, a holiday and any access to alcohol being denied him. Once again,

At the Races, 1899
Canvas, 46 x 55 cm
Albi, Musée Toulouse-Lautrec

Berthe Sarrazin was placed in charge of Lautrec, travelling to Neuilly to visit him and reporting back to the Comtesse. On 13 April she wrote to her mistress: 'I've just seen Monsieur Henri. He is still the same, rather better, above all very calm. He welcomed me and was very pleased to see me ... I took some coffee, chocolate drops

and handkerchiefs ... I didn't take the rum, as Madame can well imagine, but I said to Monsieur that I brought it but that the concierge took it from me on my way in.' Four days later she reported to the Comtesse again: 'I went to see Monsieur Henri this morning, as I didn't receive a letter from Madame ... He finds that time drags. I took him what he requested, lavender water, chocolate, coffee, butter biscuits, powdered cinnamon, lemon syrup, the six remaining handkerchiefs and four pairs of socks. I found Monsieur very well. He had never seemed more rational. He spoke very kindly of Madame and of his grandmother. He was very concerned to discover that she was worse ...' And on 20 April she wrote that she had delivered a pot of marmalade to Monsieur Henri. He '... no longer speaks badly of Madame as he had done, which proves that he is becoming completely rational ...'

The few letters that Lautrec himself wrote while in the sanatorium reveal his lucidity but at the same time his misgivings about being in such a place effectively against his will. In a letter written at the end of April or the beginning of May 1899 to his mother, who by this time had returned to Paris, Lautrec stated '... I am continuing to bear my misfortune with patience. Think about my commissions, and come to see me often. The prisoner ...'

The critics

While Lautrec was in Dr Sémelaigne's clinic at Neuilly, the Parisian press was rife with speculation about what had happened to him. It was rumoured that he was dead, or that he had gone to the clinic to die, and the newspapers were full of articles that read like obituaries, summing up his achievements and lamenting his early death. Although Lautrec was to live for a further two-and-a-half years, these articles establish the tenor for much of his posthumous reputation, and demonstrate that much of the legendary aspect that surrounds him was established by his contemporaries while he was still alive.

The critic Alexandre Hepp, writing in *Le Journal* on 26 March 1899, reported with no little relish about the artist's decline: 'Toulouse-Lautrec's friends say that they are not surprised, that it should finish in this way, Toulouse-Lautrec has the vocation for a clinic. He was locked up there yesterday, and now it is his madness which has been unmasked, that will officially sign his pictures, his drawings, his posters where it went undiscovered for so long.' Hepp subscribed to the prevalent romantic notion in conflating Lautrec's work and personality, seeing the one as the necessary outcome of the other. Other critics were not so vindictive in their assessment of Lautrec's situation, but still managed to lay the foundation for a number of subsequent myths. Two days after Hepp's article, the critic Lepelletier wrote that he was sorry to discover that Lautrec had recently been admitted to a clinic, and grieved at his rapid decline. He continued: 'An original and powerful artist, Toulouse-Lautrec had – alas! already it's necessary when speaking about him, to use the past tense of the obituary columns – quickly acquired an adequate reputation. Not prolific, a seeker, a dreamer, he thought for

Partie de Campagne, 1897
Lithograph, 40 x 57 cm

Jockey on his Way to the Scales,
1899
Lithograph, 40.2 x 29 cm

a long time about each composition, and only began work after careful premeditation ... It is regrettable that this artist, so fortunately gifted, has produced so little ...'

Lepelletier commented on Lautrec's low output; this was odd, given his relatively short career, which had begun properly only in 1882 when he went to Paris as an art student. Moreover, Lautrec had become successful only at the end of the 1880s when he started exhibiting and selling works at home and abroad on a regular basis. His first popular success had come only as recently as 1891 when he produced his first poster *At the Moulin Rouge: La Goulue* (see p. 60). In fact, at the time of his death in 1901, Lautrec left behind over 700 oil paintings and over 5,000 drawings. His was an astonishingly prolific career. The number of works he produced was similar to that of Cézanne, who died five years later, but who had been working since the end of the 1850s. Certainly Lautrec's major paintings were less numerous, and the finished, highly composed scenes, such as *Dance at the Moulin de la Galette* of 1889 (see p. 48) and *The Salon at the rue des Moulins* of 1894 (see p. 130) are relatively few, but Lepelletier was guilty of judging Lautrec's works by outmoded academic principles which would have consigned a powerful work such as *Mlle Lucie Bellanger* (see p. 138) to the status of a mere sketch and hence not really to be included in the artist's

oeuvre. However, by the turn of the century such a distinction was clearly being challenged, and Lautrec's talent can best be observed in some of his less 'finished' works; similarly the issue of prints and posters, which were considered 'popular' work and therefore not properly 'art' and whose significance could therefore be overlooked in any assessment of the artist's productivity.

That Lepelletier made such a distinction between the finished complex oil paintings and the other, much more numerous works is quite clear when he talks about Lautrec's practice, casting him as a contemplative dreamer who worked slowly and methodically. This kind of Symbolist language – the dreamer, the seeker – was in fact demonstrably false. When one looks at the rapidity and fluency of works such as *The Laundryman* (see p. 122) it is clear the critic can only be thinking of large, finished pictures when he made this pronouncement.

Lepelletier wound up: '... he was a hunch-backed Don Juan, in search of the ideal amongst the most vulgar of realities', subscribing to Hepp's notions which confuse the individual with the work, and in effect idealising Lautrec's artistic quest, suggesting that he was in search of the essential nature of humanity in his sordid depictions of reality. That Lautrec was characterised as the libertine of Spanish legend helps pinpoint the establishment of another part of the stereotypical baggage that has accompanied his posthumous reputation.

Writing in *Le Figaro* of 30 March 1899, Arsène Alexandre attempted to counter the rumours that had been circulating Paris about Lautrec. He warned: '... not a single Parisian took the trouble to find out if he was still alive before pronouncing his funeral oration ... In the public eye, in the private societies, a legend has already been formed, no one has verified it ...' Alexandre was aware of the creation of half-truths that rapidly become established as doctrine. He was sensitive to the problem of distinguishing between the given facts of the works and Lautrec's private life and continued: 'If one only considered his work, Toulouse-Lautrec did not only produce good things but also some which were incredibly beautiful. He was accessible to passers-by who could ascertain that he had renewed the art of the poster. His huge placards, treated with a well researched simplicity of lines and tones, will eventually become collectors' items, and documents that epitomise a period in history, and works of art in their own right ...' Alexandre observed the distinction between high and popular culture but prophesied that Lautrec's prints would eventually be found to preserve an intrinsic worth that would place them on a par with the more finished oil paintings. He also recognised that these popular prints, more so than the highly finished works, would eventually be held to encapsulate a whole era, the *Fin de siècle,* which demonstrates that even during the 1890s there were those who felt that the decade was marked off as being different from what had preceded it, not only in terms of the perceived gaiety and decadence but also for the political realities of anarchist bombs and the injustices of the Dreyfus affair. Whether it was in fact an essentially different time or simply construed as such by contemporary and historical accounts is open to debate.

The Jockey, 1899
Lithograph, 51.5 x 36 cm

Facsimile reproductions of the
drawing series *At the Circus*
published by Manzi-Joyant, Paris 1905

'I have bought my freedom with my drawings'

In Dr Sémelaigne's clinic Lautrec's health improved quickly. He was provided with drawing materials and lithographic stones, and in the two-and-a-half months that he was there he produced some remarkably accomplished works, apparently completely from memory. His friend Maurice Joyant suggested that he might like to make a series of drawings that could be published as an album. In the introduction to the publication of the album of twenty-two circus subjects in 1905, after Lautrec's death, Arsène Alexandre describes how his room at the hospital was turned into an artist's studio. The works draw on his early paintings of equestrian subjects and demonstrate his visual memory and thorough early training.

It seems possible that although Lautrec did not have reference to the model for these works, he may have visited the equestrian Cirque Molier in the rue Bénouville near the clinic, accompanied by one of the staff. This circus was famous for bare-back riding and several of the drawings suggest that the kind of riding skills he saw there might have influenced works such as *At the Circus: Bare-back Rider* (see p. 171). Founded in 1880 by Ernest Molier, this circus was usually associated with the *haute école* techniques and two famous horsewomen, Blanche Allarty and Anne Bradbury, and Molier himself performed a variety of skilful and daring feats. Other attractions included tight-rope walkers (see p. 174) and acrobats (see p. 178).

The works are executed in pencil, sanguine and crayon and some of them are a variety of monotype which had been favoured by Degas. The works are very different from his earliest work with a circus theme – *At the Cirque Fernando: The Equestrienne* (see p. 50) – which is only partly explained by their difference in purpose. There is no attempt in the later work to create a sense of the circus atmosphere; in the drawings the focus is on the artistes themselves, often concentrating on the kind of contortions that they underwent in the course of their performance. Joyant, usually a reliable witness, relates how after leaving the sanatorium on 20 May 1899 Lautrec confided with relief, 'I have bought my freedom with my drawings.'

At the Circus: Bear Performing,
1899
Drawing, 27.3 x 19.7 cm

165

*At the Circus: Equestrian
Acrobatics,* 1899
Drawing, 18.8 x 26.4 cm

At the Circus: The Spanish Walk,
1899
Drawing, 26.4 x 18.3 cm

At the Circus: Performing Horses,
1899
Drawing, 19.8 x 26.2 cm

At the Circus: Performing Horse,
1899
Drawing, 26.1 x 18.5 cm

At the Circus: Haute Ecole - Pointage, 1899
Drawing, 24.8 x 18.7 cm

At the Circus: Bare-back Rider, 1899
Drawing, 26.2 x 18 cm

172

At the Circus: Jockey, 1899
Drawing, 20 x 27.4 cm

At the Circus: Female Trainer, 1899
Drawing, 23.2 x 16.4 cm

Following pages

174
At the Circus: Tight-rope Walker,
1899
Drawing, 27.6 x 18.7 cm

175
At the Circus: Entering the Ring,
1899
Drawing, 27.6 x 17.8 cm

175

At the Circus: Curtain Call, 1899
Drawing, 26.1 x 18.7 cm

At the Circus: Performing Elephant, 1899
Drawing, 24.5 x 18.5 cm

177

At the Circus: Clown Trainer, 1899
Drawing, 16.6 x 27.1 cm

Previous pages

178
At the Circus: Circus Acrobats,
1899
Drawing, 27.6 x 19 cm

179
*At the Circus: Equestrienne Riding
'En Panneau',* 1899
Drawing, 27.4 x 20.9 cm

180
At the Circus: The Pas de Deux,
1899
Drawing, 26.4 x 18.8 cm

181
At the Circus: The Flying Trapeze,
1899
Drawing, 28.3 x 18.1 cm

*At the Circus: Clown Training a
Horse and Monkey,* 1899
Drawing, 26.8 x 17 cm

At the Circus: The Tandem, 1899
Drawing, 26.4 x 18.5 cm

At the Circus: Taking a Bow, 1899
Drawing, 24.5 x 18.8 cm

Chapter 9

The final years

Lautrec was released from Dr Sémelaigne's clinic by 20 May 1899, and from there went to Albi with his cousin Louis Pascal (see p. 118). His mother prevailed upon another distant cousin, Paul Viaud (see p. 190), a native of Bordeaux, to be his constant companion at this time. One of Viaud's chief virtues seems to have been that he did not drink alcohol, although it is clear from his letters that Lautrec quickly fell back into his habit of regular drinking. In a letter to his cousin Raoul Tapié de Céleyran in the summer of 1899 Lautrec wrote: 'You ask me what I'd like! Some wine. Besides, we'll drink it together, I hope. Here's what I'll do. I'm going to see some samples of red wine. I shall tell you the prices, and you can send me the number of bottles that you would like. Not much, but good quality.'

Except for a few rare trips to Paris, Lautrec was never really to return to the capital for any length of time, although he maintained the studio in the avenue Frochot which he had taken in 1897. In a visit that he made in the autumn of 1899 he discovered that the kind of speculative notices that had appeared in the Parisian press in the spring when he was at Neuilly had meant that the amounts commanded by his works had risen considerably as people invested in them. His absence from his old haunts must also have fuelled anticipation about the imminence of his death.

One old friend who remained sympathetic was Jane Avril, who commissioned a poster from Lautrec in 1899 (see p. 70). This design is sometimes used by those who wish to demonstrate Lautrec's derangement to point to the hallucinatory quality of his work at this time. Certainly, it is quite different from earlier representations of the artiste (see p. 66). Her hat – always an important feature of Avril's costume – seems like a piece of outlandish vegetation, pulling her head out of the picture space, and the serpent coiling up and round her body had no apparent basis in her act. Yet the whole thing is in keeping with the undulating rhythms of the popular Art Nouveau style and the juxtaposition of woman and snake, with its connotations of *femme fatale*, was not unusual subject-matter for the Symbolists. In the end, no poster was ever printed.

In fact, the subject of Jane Avril was exceptional in Lautrec's *oeuvre*. Other works from this period show his return to old themes. *Woman at her Toilet: Mme Poupoule* of 1899 (see p. 154) marks a return to the subject-matter of *Poudre de Riz* (see p. 46), with a woman sitting at her dressing table, which he had continued in works such as *A Passing Fancy* (see p. 132). For other artists this would have represented an opportunity to explore the glamorising and voyeuristic relationship between the depicted woman and the spectator, but for Lautrec the anonymity of the woman, her hair largely obscuring her face, and her failure to engage with anyone outside the picture space, make for a much more introspective portrayal.

The Milliner, 1900
Panel, 61 x 49.3 cm
Albi, Musée Toulouse-Lautrec

Also, he has used the same rich and densely packed colours that were evident in *At the Rat Mort* (see p. 148), effectively dismissing any suggestion that these later works were inferior to his earlier compositions.

In marked contrast, *The Englishwoman at 'The Star', Le Havre* (see p. 156) is painted in fluid, delicate colours. This oil painting depicts 'Miss Dolly', the singer from the Star café-concert in the rue Général Faidherbe in Le Havre, which was frequented by sailors. Lautrec stopped at Le Havre, where he boarded *Le Chili*, bound for Taussat with Viaud, as part of his recuperation.

Horse racing

Lautrec's early interest in equestrian subject-matter had been renewed in 1899, partly because of his friendship with Calmèse, the owner of a livery stable in Paris, but more recently in the illustrations of the circus subject-matter he had produced while in the clinic at Neuilly. Later that year he produced some of his last lithographs, drawn for an intended series of racecourse subjects, to be published as an album entitled *Les Courses* by Pierrefort, who had suggested the project when he visited the artist at Neuilly. In the end, the series was never completed and only four were printed, including *The Jockey* (see p. 162). Quite different from the early hunting scenes, worked in thickly impasted oil, these works, in their economy of line and daringly foreshortened rear ends of horses, owe their most immediate debt to the work of Degas. The interest in pattern-making (the echoing of the jockeys' bodies and the balancing of positive and negative shapes) and in flattening makes this work closer to some of Lautrec's first lithographs, with the superficially decorative qualities of works such as *Partie de Campagne* of 1897 (see p. 161) being banished in favour of a much more vivid and arresting image. (This lithograph had been published by the famous dealer Ambroise Vollard in an edition of one hundred in the second volume of his *Album des Peintres-Graveurs*.) *The Jockey* was the only one from the projected series that was eventually published by Pierrefort in two editions, monochrome and colour. Others intended for the same series, such as *Jockey on his Way to the Scales* (see p. 160) were only posthumously published by other dealers.

Horse racing was, of course, an aristocratic sport and when gambling at racecourses was outlawed in 1887, the takings plummeted. This ruling was overturned in 1891, some of the profit being given to charity, but the sport retained its aspect of élitism, being regarded as a leisure pursuit of the rich. It was widely acknowledged that the Jockey Club, founded in 1833, was the most exclusive club in Paris. At the same time, however, the government lent its support to horse breeding, which was regarded as being in the national interest, with particularly important application for military use. Lautrec's social mobility, from the popular cabarets of Montmartre to the fashionable brothels and clubs of the Grands Boulevards and the Champs-Elysées, was further enhanced by his move to the racecourses of France, with their wealthy spectators, as in *At the Races* (see p. 158).

Maurice Joyant, 1900
Panel, 116.5 x 81 cm
Albi, Musée Toulouse-Lautrec

189

190

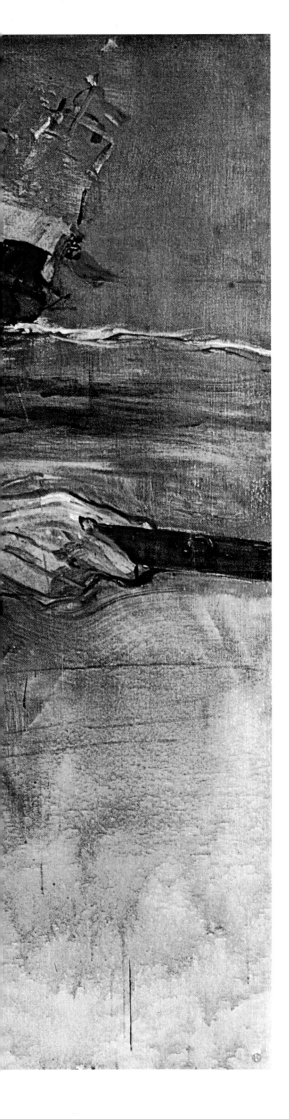

Bordeaux

Most of the remaining two years of Lautrec's life was spent in Bordeaux, Viaud's native city, in south-west France. He took a studio there and his best late works show a marked preference for portraiture, partly because his life seems to have revolved less around social environments where the temptation to drink would have been present, and partly as a record of those friends to whom he was close at this time. His hobbies now focused on sailing and deep-sea fishing. In a letter to his mother, written in the summer of 1899 from Taussat-les-Bains near Arcachon, he reported: 'I've lost one of my cormorants who must have regretted leaving me, because the inhabitants of Audegne greeted him with a round of gunfire and his body was strewn all over the ground ...' It was as a cormorant hunter that Lautrec painted the portrait of his boyhood friend *Maurice Joyant* in 1900 (see p. 188). Apparently, the work took seventy-two sittings before Lautrec was satisfied with it, but there is no sense of laboured execution in this painting in dilute oil on panel. In some places, particularly noticeable on the right-hand side, the paint is so thin that it has trickled down the surface of the wood like water-colour.

A portrait of *Viaud as an English Admiral* (see p. 190) was found in the dining-room of his mother's home at Malromé after Lautrec's death. A kind of costume piece, with his friend dressed in the outfit of an eighteenth-century admiral, directing the sailing ship at the top of the picture space with his baton, it demonstrates Lautrec's love of theatricality.

The sonorous tonality of one of his last portraits, *An Examination at the Faculty of Medicine, Paris* (see p. 194), is reminiscent of a Rembrandt both in its medical subject-matter and in its use of light and shade to heighten the mood of the work. In it, Lautrec has depicted his cousin Gabriel Tapié de Céleyran on the left-hand side as he presents his medical thesis to Professors Wurtz and Fournier. As this had taken place in 1899, the painting is simply a reconstruction of the event, probably intended as a gift for Wurtz, in whose family the work remained until it passed to the Toulouse-Lautrec museum in Albi.

The discernibly darker palette coupled with the interest in light and shade which was first noticeable in, for example, *At the Rat Mort* of 1899 (see p. 148) is particularly evident in *The Milliner* (see p. 186). The woman, her head ablaze with reds and greens, marks a further instance of Lautrec's use of a red-haired model, which he had favoured in early works such a *Woman with Red Hair in the Garden of Père Forest* (see p. 40) or the more recent *La Toilette* (see p. 136). She is glimpsed at work across a particularly magnificent hat in the foreground, with a pair of hats on stands in the background, isolated and yet with no suggestion of the boredom

Viaud as an English Admiral,
1900-1901
Canvas, 139 x 153 cm
São Paulo, Museu de Arte

or drudgery that had characterised Lautrec's much earlier depiction of a working woman, *The Laundress* (see p. 30). The glowing figure of the milliner seen against the sombre background and the crisp line of her profile lend the work the quality of an icon.

Messaline

Lautrec's forays into the world of the respectable theatre had been few, most notably in his depiction of Sarah Bernhardt (see p. 94), but in the winter of 1900–1901, he produced a series of paintings of a production of Jacques Offenbach's *La Belle Hélène* and of Isidore de Lara's tragic operetta *Messaline*. The latter had its début in Bordeaux in 1900 and Lautrec produced six paintings of it as well as a number of sketches. He wrote to Joyant asking for photographs of the work to help with his paintings. These all concentrate on the leading lady, Mlle Ganne, who played the Empress. In the most impressive *Messaline Descending the Staircase* (p. 192) Lautrec has returned to the use of reds and greens that he had explored in recent works, so that the scarlet of her dress is surrounded by cool bluish greens. The bulky figure of the soldier in the foreground acts as a *repoussoir* element, focusing attention into the brightly illuminated middle distance, a device Lautrec had used in a number of earlier works, most notably *At the Moulin Rouge: La Goulue* (see p. 60). These paintings were Lautrec's last sustained attempt at any major works and provide a fitting climax to his artistic career. In April of 1901 he returned to Paris accompanied by Viaud, apparently to put his studio and effects in order and left it for the last time on 15 July. While he was at Taussat-les-Bains near Arcachon he was overcome by an attack of paralysis which left him unable to walk and almost totally deaf. He returned to his mother at Malromé where he died on 9 September 1901.

In an obituary that appeared in *La Dépêche de Toulouse* on 9 September 1901, the writer Baragnon pointed out that Lautrec's reputation had been moulded by the Parisian press, who constructed a persona for him that had little basis in his art and a great deal to do with his appearance:
'Because he was small, ugly, paradoxical, and in every way unique, the Parisians, always hasty to judge everyone simply on his appearance, made of Lautrec a neat little conception – a schema. He was the prisoner of a formula. The words gnome, dwarf, bohemian of Montmartre, lend themselves to the pen of the obituary writers. They conveyed only one side of this misunderstood nature, which remained despite the disgraces, at heart as noble as his birth.'
Other notices, such as the one that appeared in the *Journal de Paris* on the following day, suggest that Lautrec encapsulated the spirit of the *fin de siècle*. What such commentators failed to appreciate was the logical error of their arguments. Instead of defining and describing something essentially different about France, and particularly Paris, at the end of the nineteenth century, Lautrec's art was used as a paradigm then as well as now, to help construct a vision of something that was decadent and hence in the throes

An Examination at the Faculty of
Medicine, Paris, 1901
Canvas, 65 x 81 cm
Albi, Musée Toulouse-Lautrec

194

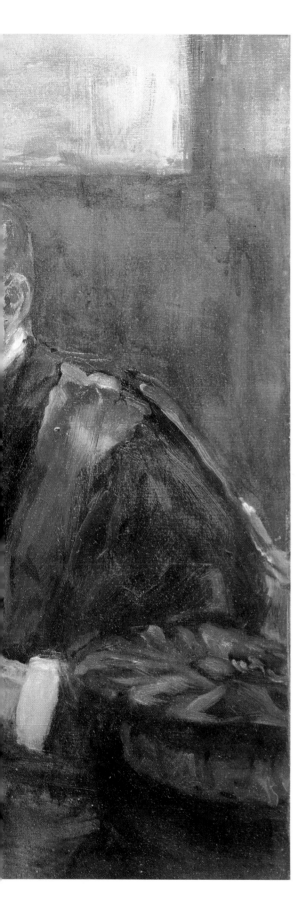

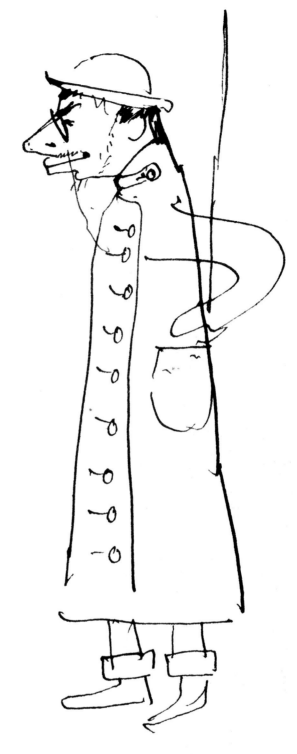

of decline. It was through Lautrec's work, particularly the popular prints, that Paris sought an identity for itself. In that respect, Lautrec's rumoured death in 1899 and his actual death in 1901 coincided neatly with the end of an era. The kind of realism, of topicality, that such writers found in his work is only possible because of his premature death. Had he lived on into the twentieth century then his reputation might have declined, as the milieu in which he moved and depicted became outmoded. In a sense, the leaps from the popular cabarets and cafés to the fashionable theatres and race tracks that provide the subject-matter for his work in the last decade of his life, demonstrate a repertoire that he adapted to suit an increasingly confident nation as France emerged into the twentieth century.

Henri de Toulouse-Lautrec, c.1885
Pen drawing, 17.5 x 11.2 cm
Albi, Musée Toulouse-Lautrec

Bibliography

Jean Adhémar, *Toulouse-Lautrec: his Complete Lithographs
and Drypoints*, London 1965

Götz Adriani (ed.), *Toulouse-Lautrec: the Complete Graphic Works*,
Royal Academy of Arts, London 1988

Matthias Arnold, *Henri de Toulouse-Lautrec 1864-1901: the Theatre
of Life*, Cologne 1987

Frances Carey and Anthony Griffiths, *From Manet to Toulouse-Lautrec,
French Lithographs 1860-1900*, London 1978

Catalogue Musée Toulouse-Lautrec, Albi 1985

Douglas Cooper, *Henri de Toulouse-Lautrec*, London 1955

Bernard Denvir, *Toulouse-Lautrec*, London 1991

M.G. Dortu, *Toulouse-Lautrec et son oeuvre*, 6 volumes, New York 1971

Lucien Goldschmidt and Herbert Schimmel, *Unpublished Correspondence of Henri de Toulouse-Lautrec*, London 1969

Edouard Julien, *Toulouse-Lautrec: Moulin Rouge*, London 1958

Jacques Lassaigne, *Toulouse-Lautrec and the Paris of the Cabarets*,
London 1989

Edward Lucie-Smith, *Toulouse-Lautrec*, London 1977

Thadée Natanson, *Un Henri de Toulouse-Lautrec*, Geneva 1951

Fritz Novotny, *Toulouse-Lautrec*, London 1969

Henri Perruchot, *Toulouse-Lautrec*, London 1960

Post-Impressionism: Cross Currents in European Painting,
Royal Academy of Arts, London 1979-80

John Rewald, *Post-Impressionism from Van Gogh to Gauguin*,
London and New York 1978

Richard Shone, *Toulouse-Lautrec*, London 1977

Richard Thomson, *Toulouse-Lautrec*, London 1977

Maria Cionini Visani, *Toulouse-Lautrec*, London 1970

Index

Photo credits

Lauros-Giraudon, Paris
Jose A. Naranjo, Washington
RMN, Paris
Stedelijk Museum, reproduction department, Amsterdam
Elke Walford, Hamburg
and the photo libraries of the collections mentioned in the captions.

The author and the publisher wish to thank the museums, galleries and private collectors for the permission to reproduce in this volume works of art from their collections.